Sweet Envy

Sweet Envy

DECEPTIVELY EASY DESSERTS,
DESIGNED TO STEAL THE SHOW

SETON ROSSINI

THE COUNTRYMAN PRESS

The Countryman Press
Woodstock, Vermont
www.countrymanpress.com

A division of W. W. Norton & Company, Inc.,
500 Fifth Avenue, New York, NY 10110
www.wwnorton.com

For information about special discounts
for bulk purchases, please contact
W.W. Norton Special Sales at
specialsales@wwnorton.com
or 800-233-4830.

Library of Congress Cataloging-in-Publication Data

Rossini, Seton.
 Sweet envy : deceptively easy desserts,
designed to steal the show / Seton Rossini.
   pages cm
 Includes index.
 ISBN 978-1-58157-278-0 (hardcover)
 1. Desserts. I. Title.

TX773.R7955 2015
641.86—dc23

                       2015009909

Printed in China

10 9 8 7 6 5 4 3 2 1

For Tom & Nolan

Contents

CITRUS CONFETTI COOKIES

Every real shindig needs confetti, right? And not the artificial kind that you'll be stuck cleaning up for weeks. Swap the boring old plastic confetti for these itty-bitty cookies and you're sure to find a reason to celebrate. You may want to practice moderation here, they're very easy to devour by the handful! Orange zest adds an unexpected citrus boost, elevating each little cookie. Now what should we celebrate today?

Short on time? Skip the cookie cutters and use a sharp knife and a ruler to cut the dough into ½-inch squares instead.

Makes about 5 cups of "confetti"

2 cups all-purpose flour
½ teaspoon baking soda
½ teaspoon salt
4 tablespoons (½ stick) unsalted butter, softened
½ cup granulated sugar
1 egg
2 teaspoons whole milk
1 teaspoon vanilla extract
2 tablespoons orange juice
1 teaspoon orange zest
Gel food coloring (at least 3 colors)
Sprinkles (optional)

Combine the flour, baking soda and salt in a small bowl and set aside.

In the bowl of a stand mixer fitted with the paddle attachment, beat the butter and sugar until light and fluffy. Add the egg, milk and vanilla, and continue to mix until incorporated.

Beat in the orange juice and zest, then add the flour mixture. Mix until dough just comes together. Divide the dough into equal parts for each color, plus a part that will remain un-tinted or "white". Wrap this part in plastic wrap and set aside.

Toss another part back into the mixer (no need to clean out the mixing bowl) and add a couple drops of food coloring. Mix on low until you have the desired shade, then wrap tightly in plastic wrap and set aside.

Repeat the coloring process with another piece of dough and additional food coloring until all of the dough has been colored and wrapped. Refrigerate the dough for at least 2 hours, or until firm.

Preheat the oven to 350°F. Line a cookie sheet with a baking liner or parchment paper and set aside.

Lightly flour your work surface and remove the dough from the refrigerator. Working with one color at a time, unwrap and roll out the dough to ⅛-inch thick.

Use the back of piping tips or small cookie cutters to create cookies no bigger than ½-inch in diameter.

Fill up the cookie sheet, making sure none of the cookies overlap, then bake for 6 to 8 minutes. Cool completely and store in an airtight container.

SUGAR & SPICE TWISTS

Puff pastry might just be the answer to all the world's problems. Aside from being incredibly easy to use, it's always delicious. The delicate buttery layers seem to melt in your mouth, leading you to question why more foods aren't wrapped in its flaky goodness. Puff pastry is perfect for last minute entertaining or if you're simply on a time crunch. *Like when you find out the book club just got relocated to your apartment and a dozen hungry people will be at your doorstep within minutes.* These twists have a real presence. They look much fancier than they actually are, making them the perfect treat for a crowd. Although I wouldn't pass judgment if you made them for a party of one. Did I mention they're filled with cinnamon, sugar, nutmeg and pecans? Enough said.

Makes 9 large twists

¼ cup granulated sugar
1 tablespoon cinnamon
1 teaspoon nutmeg
1 package (2 sheets) pre-made puff pastry, thawed
3 tablespoons unsalted butter, melted
¾ cup chopped pecans

Preheat the oven to 400°F and line two baking sheets with baking liners or parchment paper. In a small bowl, combine the sugar, cinnamon, and nutmeg and set aside.

Lightly flour your work surface, unfold and roll the two sheets of puff pastry to a 9-by-12-inch rectangles.

Generously butter the top side of each sheet. Cover one sheet with the sugar mixture and sprinkle it with pecans. Then carefully place the other sheet, butter side down, on top. Lightly roll to press the two sheets together.

Use a sharp knife to cut nine 1-by-12-inch strips, then arrange on the baking sheets.

Working with one strip at a time, grab the ends and twist in opposite directions to form a tight spiral.

Lightly press the ends into the baking sheet to keep them from separating. Bake for 15 to 20 minutes, or until the twists are golden. Cool slightly before serving.

CHOCO-NAÑA TART

The combination of bananas and chocolate, specifically Nutella, is undoubtedly one of the finest pairings in the history of dessert. I love the chance to add fruit into my dessert regimen, as it makes me feel a little better about the massive amounts of chocolate I consume. This tart is absolutely gorgeous and takes just minutes to assemble. It only contains five ingredients, making it a hassle-free dessert to serve when entertaining. Its simplicity is a testament to the power of bananas and chocolate.

Makes one 14-by-6-inch tart

6 bananas
3 tablespoons granulated sugar
2 teaspoons lemon juice
½ package (1 sheet) pre-made puff pastry, thawed
½ cup Nutella

Peel the bananas and slice on a sharp diagonal into ½-inch-thick pieces. Combine the bananas, sugar and lemon juice in a bowl, making sure to coat each banana slice.

Preheat the oven to 400°F and line a baking sheet with a liner or parchment paper.

Lightly flour your work surface and without unfolding the puff pastry, roll the dough into a 16-by-8-inch rectangle. Transfer the puff pastry to the baking sheet and prick the dough several times with a fork.

Spread the Nutella evenly on the dough, leaving a 2-inch border.

Arrange the banana slices on top of the Nutella, creating rows that slightly overlap.

Fold over the edges of the puff pastry, then bake for 30 minutes, or until the edges are golden brown. Cool slightly before serving.

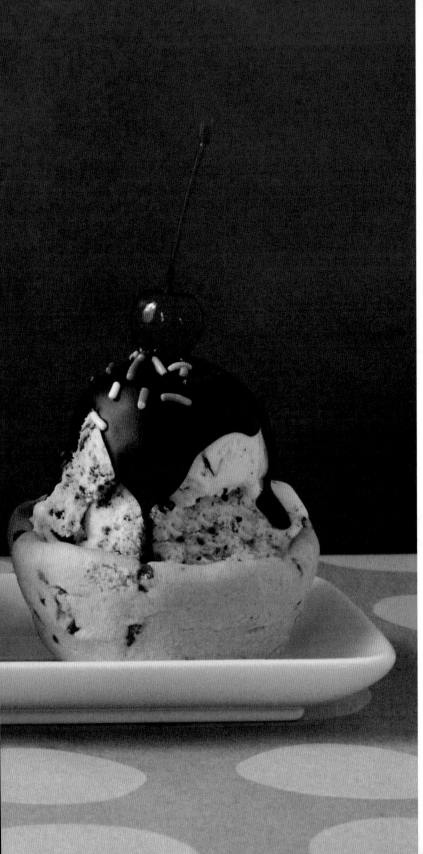

While the majority of this cookbook is devoted to sweet treats (*and rightfully so!*) I'd be remiss if I didn't shine a small light on the importance of entertaining in style. A decadent layer cake deserves to be displayed on a beautiful platter; a plain old dinner plate isn't doing justice to your hard work in the kitchen. It's like macaroni without the cheese, bacon without eggs—it just doesn't make sense. Never underestimate the importance of being a crafty host. (*Read: Don't miss out on a real chance to impress your guests.*)

Cooking for guests is half the battle, and being a prepared host is just as important. I know you're thinking, "You expect me to bake all these delicious treats and find time to D.I.Y.!?" Yes, I do expect that of you—mostly because these projects are incredibly simple—plus, the payoff is big. It's the small things that make a lasting impression. Create an inspiring cake stand or two, or 100. Craft projects can be edible, too: Swap your sugar cubes for the molded sugar letters, and you might just be the coolest person you know. (*Not that that would surprise you.*)

SUGAR LETTERS

D.I.Y. CAKE STAND

SUGAR COOKIE GIFT TAGS

LEAF PLACE CARD HOLDERS

CHALKBOARD CHARGERS

COOKIE CUP SUNDAES

SUGAR LETTERS

Sure, a spoonful of sugar sweetens your cup of coffee or tea, but these molded sugar letters are just as sweet and much more festive! This is where you can get really creative as a hostess. Sugar letters can replace the traditional name card at a shower or tea party. Line your saucers with the names of your guests, or just serve them in a sugar dish for an added playful touch at your event. Keep it simple by molding initials or heart shapes. Mold the sugar letters a couple days in advance. Once they dry they're just like sugar cubes—only better.

TIP

Purist at heart?
Keep the sugar white
and the letters will
look just as beautiful,
especially if you have
colorful teacups.

YOU'LL NEED:
Sugar Letters recipe (see recipe)
Gel food coloring (optional)
Small alphabet cookie cutters

SUGAR LETTERS
1 to 4 cups of superfine granulated sugar (1 cup is needed for each color)
¼ cup of water (per color)

Place sugar in a mixing bowl. Slowly add in the water, one teaspoon at a time, stirring thoroughly until the sugar resembles wet sand.

The sugar is ready when you squeeze it in your hand and large clumps form. Equally divide sugar into separate small bowls, one for each color.

Add the food coloring one drop at time, stirring until you get the preferred color.

Line a baking sheet with a liner or parchment paper and pour the sugar out onto the sheet. Use your palm to flatten the sugar until it's an even ¼-inch thick. If the sugar doesn't stick together, sprinkle a few drops of water and continue to mold it.

Use the cookie cutters to cut out sugar letters. Let dry for about two hours. You can re-use all the leftover sugar by sprinkling it with water and reforming it again.

Desserts look a little more irresistible when they're elevated on a cute little pedestal. And since cake stands can get pricey, making them yourself is both cost effective and creative. I, for one, have had an obsession with cake stands since I started making cakes. Somehow, I've slowly evolved into the cat lady of cake stands—I have dozens of them. The idea for a D.I.Y. cake stand revealed itself to me one day at a thrift store when I stumbled upon an entire set of olive green retro dinnerware. These dishes were a throwback to the '70s, clearly having had their moment in the days of fondue parties and shag carpets. They were perfect. I stacked the dishes and goblets to carry them over to the cash register and I was delighted when I noticed how perfectly a salad plate rested upon a wine goblet. The real thrill in making these cake stands is sourcing the plates and glasses. The best dinnerware—found at thrift stores or in your great-aunt's attic—is filled with character and has a story to tell. Look for an interesting goblet, with a strong enough neck to hold the weight of a cake. The plate can be anything from a basic round dish to an elaborate scallop-edged platter. Once it's all painted, you can give it a unified custom look.

D.I.Y. CAKE STAND

YOU'LL NEED:
Assorted goblets and plates
Glue (I use E600)
Non-toxic spray paint and craft paint
Small paintbrushes and paint for detail work (optional)
Clear food-safe shellac (I use Zinsser Bulls Eye Shellac)

Clean and dry the plates and goblets before gluing. Glue the goblet base to the bottom of your plate of choice, then let it set.

Spray the cake stand with the non-toxic spray paint. It will likely take two coats; be sure to let the paint dry completely in between coats.

Add some detail! Whether it's gold trim or polka dots, showcase your personal style with smaller paintbrushes and a complementary paint color.

Seal in your handiwork with a clear food-safe shellac; let dry completely before using. Wipe them clean after each use or hand wash only.

SUGAR COOKIE GIFT TAGS

If the gift you're giving isn't edible, then at least the tag should be. (*The giftee won't even care what's in the box once she tastes the gift tag.*) To make them, simply decorate a classic sugar cookie with royal icing and a few sprinkles. A punched hole and a decorative ribbon turn them into gift tags. They could also double as place cards or Christmas ornaments, just make sure to hang them high enough so your four-legged friends don't eat them all.

YOU'LL NEED:
Sugar Cookie Dough (see recipe)
Gift Tag Template (pg. 160)
Royal Icing (see recipe)
Assorted sprinkles and crushed candy canes
Colorful ribbon
Small, flat cellophane gift bags (optional)

Makes 18 tags

SUGAR COOKIE DOUGH
2 cups all-purpose flour
½ teaspoon baking powder
½ teaspoon salt
4 tablespoons (½ stick) unsalted butter, softened
½ cup granulated sugar
1 egg
1 teaspoon vanilla extract
2 tablespoons whole milk

ROYAL ICING
4 cups (about 1 lb.) confectioners' sugar
3 tablespoons meringue powder
¼ cup water
1 teaspoon vanilla, almond, or lemon extract
Gel food coloring

Combine the flour, baking powder and salt in a small bowl and set aside.

In a stand mixer fitted with the paddle attachment, beat the butter and sugar until light and fluffy. Add the egg and vanilla and continue to mix until incorporated.

Beat in the milk, then add the flour mixture. Mix until dough just comes together. Wrap dough in plastic wrap and refrigerate for at least 2 hours, or until firm.

Preheat the oven to 350°F. Line a baking sheet with a liner or parchment paper and cut out the gift tag templates.

Roll out the chilled dough on a floured work surface to about ⅛-inch thick. Use a sharp knife to cut around the template, and carefully place the cookies 1 inch apart on the baking sheet.

Gather and re-roll scraps to make more cookies. Use a straw to punch a hole in the top of each tag.

Bake for 10 minutes or until the edges turn golden brown. Let cool.

Combine the sugar, meringue powder, water and vanilla in the bowl of a stand mixer fitted with the whisk attachment and beat until icing is shiny and soft peaks form.

The consistency is right when you remove the whisk attachment and the peaks falls onto themselves. If icing is too thick, add more water, one teaspoon at a time. If it's too runny, add more confectioners' sugar.

Depending on how many colors you want, divide the icing evenly into small bowls and color with food coloring. Once colored, scoop icing into piping bag fitted with a size 3 tip.

To Assemble:
Use a small offset spatula to spread royal icing on the top one-third of the cookie, then cover with sprinkles or crushed candy canes.

To personalize, pipe a name or message in royal icing and set aside to harden.

Once dry, carefully loop a ribbon through the hole and tie the tag to a wrapped gift. If your gift will be handled a lot, place the cookie in a flat cellophane gift bag before attaching.

LEAF PLACE CARD HOLDERS

Leaf molds are clearly a favorite of mine (see Chocolate Mint Leaves on pg. 101). They're incredibly simple and add a bit of rustic sophistication. A brush of gold paint around the edges makes these place card holders luxe, but they're made from the easy-to-use kid's air-dry clay. (*It'll be our little secret.*) Finding leaves for the molds is an adventure in itself. Maple leaves are perfect for Thanksgiving or fall get-togethers; a large hydrangea leaf lends itself to an outdoor garden party or summer shindig.

YOU'LL NEED:

Rolling pin
Air-dry clay (I use Crayola)
Sharp knife
Craft paint (I used leaf green and gold)
Paintbrush

Roll out the clay to ⅛-inch thick on a nonstick surface. Place the leaf (back-side down) on the clay and press in so the veins of the leaf make an impression in the clay.

Use a sharp knife to cut around the perimeter of the leaf, then peel away the leaf and remove the excess clay. Use your fingers to mold up the edges of the clay into a slight dish shape. Let air-dry for a couple of days.

Roughly brush the edges of the clay with the paint, then let dry completely before using. Display a name card inside each leaf. To clean, just wipe them off with a damp towel.

TIP: Look for a healthy leaf with an interesting and pronounced vein pattern.

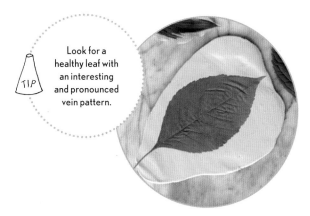

CHALKBOARD CHARGERS

Dust off those old chargers and bring them back to the dinner table. With a touch of matte black chalkboard paint, these chargers get personal— well, *personalized*. The black adds a dramatic pop to your table and the chalkboard finish means you can customize each charger. Whether you write guests' names, a menu, or even a simple holiday message, the possibilities are endless.

YOU'LL NEED:
Basic chargers
2-inch-wide paintbrush
Painter's tape
Chalkboard paint
Chalk

Wipe the chargers to make sure they're clean, then section off the top third of the plate with painter's tape. Repeat with all of the chargers.

Use the paintbrush to brush an even coat of paint on the top third of the plate and set aside to dry. Each charger will need two coats of paint.

Once they're dry, carefully remove the painter's tape and grab some chalk to customize. Wipe them clean after each use or hand wash only.

TIP

Add ¼ cup of sprinkles for a more colorful cookie dough.

COOKIE CUP SUNDAES

Ice cream sundaes are pretty much perfect as is. Although they can vary, a traditional sundae combines creamy ice cream smothered in a gooey chocolate fudge sauce and topped with a maraschino cherry. Sprinkles, of course, are always encouraged. The only thing you can do to improve an ice cream sundae is to toss it in a delicious peanut butter chocolate chip cookie. An edible bowl? Now, we've achieved the perfect ice cream sundae. These cookie bowls are not only incredibly impressive, they make for an easy clean-up. Now, if we could just find a way to eat the spoon, too.

Makes 18 cookie cups

2 cups all-purpose flour
½ teaspoon baking soda
½ teaspoon salt
½ cup (1 stick) butter, softened
½ cup light brown sugar
½ cup granulated sugar
1 egg
1 teaspoon vanilla extract
½ cup creamy peanut butter
¼ cup mini chocolate chips

Preheat the oven to 375°F. Grease the bottom of a 12-cup muffin pan and set aside.

In a bowl, combine the flour, baking soda and salt, then set aside.

Using a stand mixer fitted with the paddle attachment, beat butter and sugars until creamy. Add the egg, beat until fully incorporated, then add the vanilla extract.

Slowly add in flour mixture, then add the peanut butter and mini chocolate chips, mixing until incorporated. Transfer dough to a floured work surface and roll to ⅛-inch thick. (If dough is too soft to roll out, chill in the refrigerator for 15 minutes.)

Use a 3-inch round cutter or an inverted cup to cut the dough into large circles. Press the dough circles onto the greased muffin pan cups, making sure that the dough wraps over and sticks to the cup.

Bake for 8 to 10 minutes or until just golden brown around the edges. Cool for 5 minutes, then gently nudge the bowls off the muffin cups. Set aside to cool completely.

Fill cup with ice cream and top with all the fixins. Resist the temptation to eat the bowl before the ice cream. If you do, you'll be left with quite a mess.

CHOCOLATE FUDGE COATING
(See recipe on pg. 54)

TEMPLATES ARE ACTUAL SIZE. PHOTOCOPY FOR REPEATED USE.

A B C D E

F G H I J

K L M N

O P Q R S

T U V W

X Y Z ! &

1 2 3 4 5

6 7 8 9 0

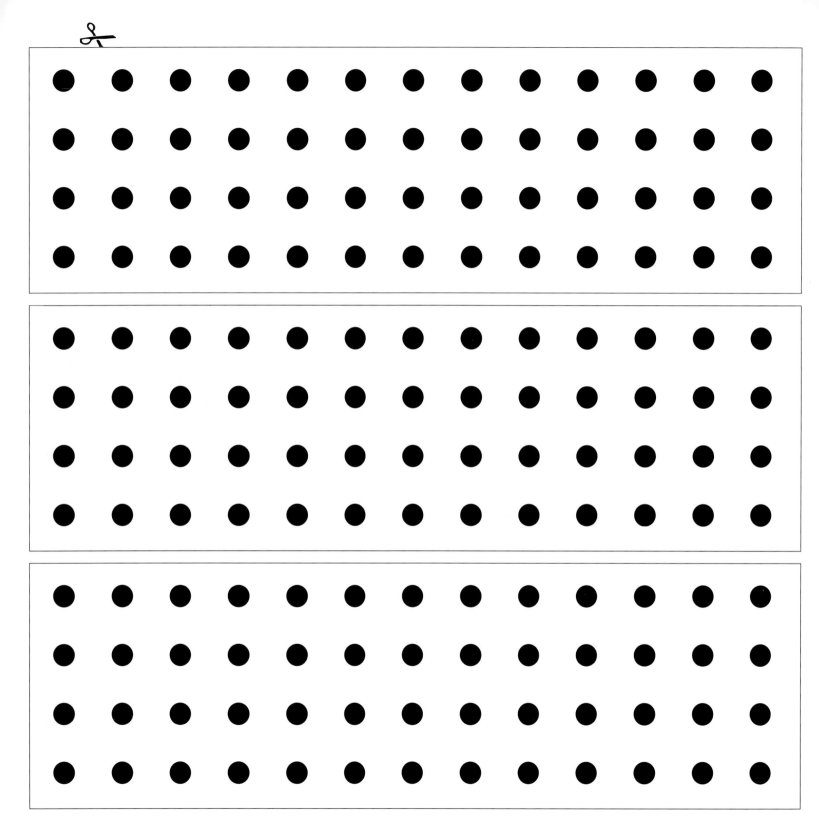

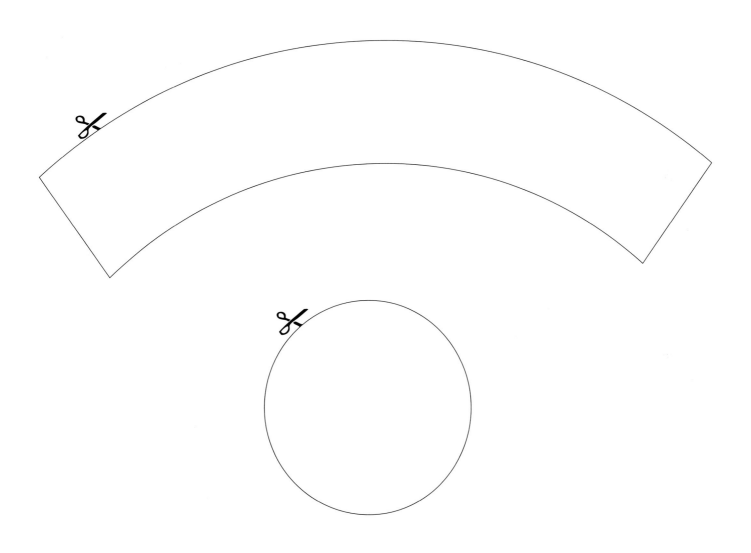

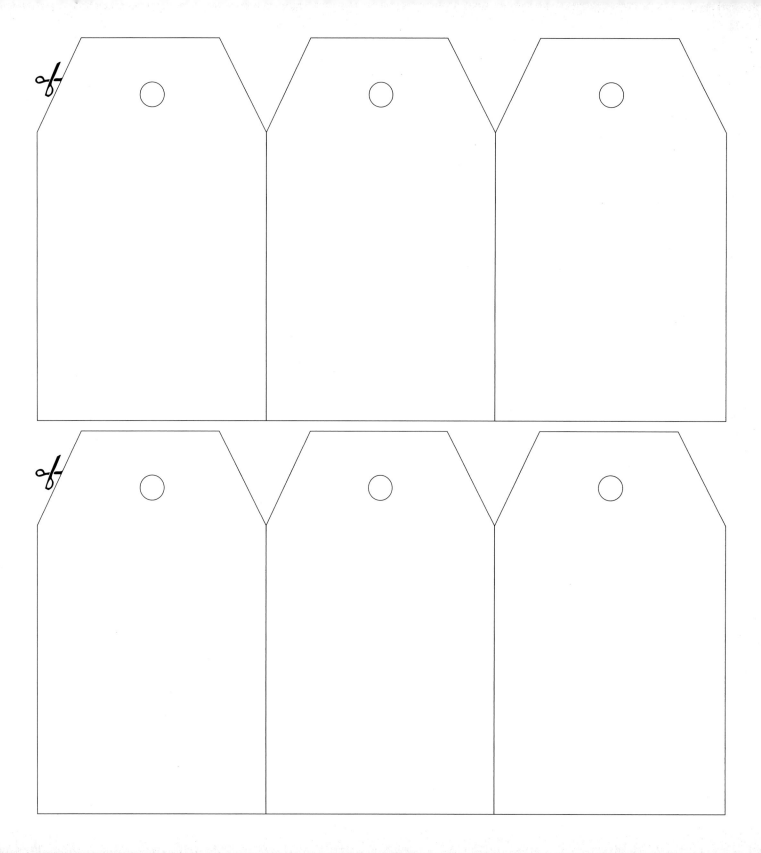

INDEX

THANKS

The pages that fill this book are the product of many creative brainstorms, sugar induced all-nighters, recipes tested 'til our bellies hurt, and hours hunched over a laptop. This incredible journey that is *Sweet Envy* wouldn't have been possible without the guidance and generosity of many people. A huge thanks goes out to Leanna Weller Smith for introducing me to Ann Treistman, my sensational editor at The Countryman Press. Thank you, Ann, for putting so much faith in me and allowing me to make the dessert book of my dreams. You and your all-star team at The Countryman Press have made this process seamless and so enjoyable.

As I learned years ago with my seventh grade cheerleading squad, a pyramid is only as strong as its base. To my base, my family and friends, you rock. Thank you Mom and Papa for endless encouragement and guidance. This includes supporting me in various activities that I would clearly never excel in (consisting of, but not limited to: Texas Gold Dance Troop, softball, and piano lessons), to eventually allowing me to follow my dreams in NYC. Thanks to my father, who is responsible for my addiction to ice cream. Papa, I'll take a drive to look at real estate any day as long as I get that ice cream cone as promised.

To my siblings, Dan, Brendan, Haley, and Devin: Although our imaginary rock band never came to fruition, I couldn't have asked for a better home team. Thanks for being honest, unapologetic taste testers, and thanks for making childhood a blast. To your spouses, Colleen, Abby, Charles, and Liz: You all are inspiring and amazing for so many reasons, but thanks mostly for putting up with us Hurson kids. Daniel, Owen, Mary, Colin, Connelly, Patrick, Tate, Desmond, and Holden: anytime you need a sugar fix, I'll be here to sneak you a cookie.

Thanks to my incredible grandparents, aunts, uncles, cousins, and second cousins alike. Thanks to Walter, Ginny, Cara, Cristy, and the entire Rossini family for welcoming me in an instant and for adding a few beloved Boston accents to my life. Your love and support are true blessings.

Thank you to *Food & Wine*, who showed me what it really means to blur the lines of work and social life. Christina Grdovic Baltz, Wendy Mure, and Rory Tischler, thank you first and foremost for making me part of an incredible team and for allowing me to grow into the sugar-obsessed creative person I am today. Dana Cowin, Gail Simmons, FWArt, Solo Cups, and the entire F&W family: You're true inspirational friends and supporters. Loved the job. Still love the team.

Kimberly Fusaro, you are my grammar fairy and I'm incredibly grateful for your thoughtful support. Eunice Choi, you're a true delight and an excellent recipe tester. Thank you to the ever-stylish and smart Scott Feldman and TwoTwelve Management for believing in me even before I did.

Tom, my wedding vows should have included a warning about the copious hours spent in the kitchen. Your sugar addiction rivals mine, and I love you for that. Thank you for always saving room for dessert and for being my best friend. To Nolan, thank you for being my sweetest creation yet. May you discover your passions with effortless joy.

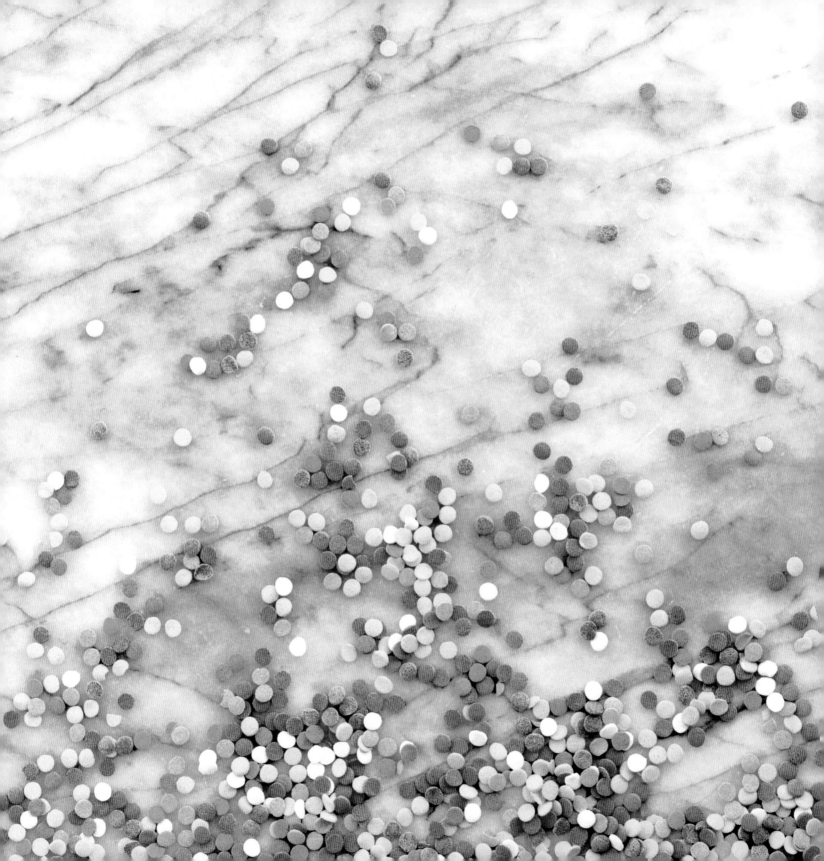

Congratulations!

Whether you're just browsing the first page in an attempt to appear dessert-savvy or you actually own this book, you have in your hands the *essential* manual to becoming a home pastry aficionado. Legally, I can't make any promises, but I can assure you that these desserts will most definitely cause jealousy among your peers. (What I like to call "sweet envy.")

The pages that follow are truly a love letter to baking. (It's not *all* just an attempt to make your friends swoon over your fancy-pants desserts.) Clearly you feel the love too, as you've almost made it to the first recipe. *Don't quit now!*

You don't need to be a trained chef to navigate this book, just bring your sweet tooth and a few mixing bowls. And as the adage goes, I hope you don't judge this book solely by its cover. If you do like the cover, thanks for the flattery, but please don't toss the book on a shelf or coffee table to sit there and look pretty. (*Full disclosure here, I'm quite guilty of superficially showcasing cookbooks because they're pretty. See: My color-coded bookshelves.*) My point is, this book is meant to be read, the recipes are meant to be made, and, most importantly, the desserts are meant to be eaten. I hope you dog-ear this book left and right, spill vanilla extract and smear egg yolk on its pages. *Sweet Envy* should proudly bear grease stains and wear, the battle wounds of a well-used cookbook.

If you're ready to create a pastry presence, this book will equip you with the techniques to impress. The confections range from sweets easy enough to bake in your sleep—*although baking in your sleep is highly unadvisable*—to cupcakes adorned with intricate fondant succulents. Whether it's a quick go-to cookie recipe, or something a bit more complex, these recipes are a solid foundation to build upon. Flip through the pages, get inspired and inevitably you'll discover a new technique that you can add to your baking arsenal.

Most importantly, make mistakes while you bake and learn from them. Stain your clothes with food coloring, get fondant and buttercream stuck in your fingernails. Know that any mistake made in the kitchen can happily be eaten. Whatever your skill level, the outcome remains the same. These are desserts that look just as amazing as they taste. Make a statement with the simple yet genuinely delicious Strawberry Shortbread Stacks (pg. 37). Get your sweet-and-salty on while celebrating candy with the Take-A-Break Bars (pg. 49). If entertaining is your thing, showcase the Piñata Cake (pg. 59) at a colorful fiesta. Impress at a sophisticated tea party with the Earl Grey Tea Cakes (pg. 41). Use unexpected flavors and colors while turning art into cake and cake into art. Daydream away as you add your own personality to a Watercolor Celebration Cake (pg. 79). With this book as your guide, you're poised to create some incredible desserts and a few show-stopping accompaniments, like the D.I.Y. Cake Stands (pg. 145). Before you realize it, you'll have garnered more than a few *oohs* and *ahhs*.

Go ahead, cause a stir with your mother-in-law or turn heads at the school bake sale. You've earned it. Flex those creative baking muscles—being envied never tasted so sweet.

BAKE IT
'TIL
YOU MAKE
IT

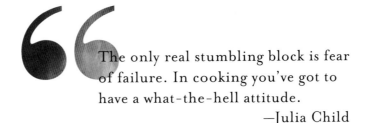

> " The only real stumbling block is fear of failure. In cooking you've got to have a what-the-hell attitude.
> —Julia Child

I n the beginning baking was a means to eat sweets whenever I wanted. I'd stand in the kitchen in a tutu and my mom's version of an apron (one of my dad's oversized button-down shirts on backwards), crafting any excuse to bake up something sugary and sweet. Eventually I outgrew that pudgy little girl phase. (And, sadly, the tutu as well.) But I still had a passion for spending time in the kitchen—the social epicenter of our family. I continued to bake in the, "Hey, I love frosting, let's go make a chocolate cake" kinda way. Not the, "I must excel at this and attend the finest pastry school in the country" way. I'm not a pastry snob, I'm a pastry lover.

Instead art and design became my career path, and after high school I fled to the Big Apple to study at Parsons School of Design (*No, not for fashion, but graphic design*), busted my ass working internships and spent endless nights hand-painting tiny color swatches that, to anyone other than my instructor, would have all been the same color blue.

Don't get me wrong, aside from probably sniffing too many chemicals and the male-to-female ratio, I loved art school and still adore everything about design. It's my profession and my passion, and because of that I never really considered my love for baking a career possibility. I considered myself a sweets superfan, baking for fun and eating everything sweet NYC had to offer.

THE CREPE EPIPHANY

It was in my senior year of college—2005, to be exact—that I had my culinary epiphany. There I was, in Union Square, right in the middle of one of those endless street fairs. Not a cool street fair that featured handmade jewelry and local goat cheese purveyors. It was one of the tourist traps that arrives and disappears in a single day, leaving heaping mounds of trash in its wake. In between classes and in need of a sweet pick-me-up, I found myself at this street fair, hopelessly wedged between a vendor selling watermelon and another dealing patterned ponchos and toenail clippers. Then I saw it: At the corner was a small French crepe stand. (*I use the word "French" loosely here, fully knowing the people who ran that stand were about as "French" as french fries.*) Naturally I ordered a Nutella and strawberry crepe, as we can all agree that Nutella is a gift from the gods, destined to be paired with sliced strawberries, all wrapped up in a cozy crepe. One taste and it hit me. It was there, on the corner of 13th and Broadway, that I had tasted my future. And it was delicious.

Maybe I was just a starving college kid, but having that delicately folded crepe changed my perception of sweets and gave me a craving to investigate baking on a deeper level. It was about the simplest thing you could have—that delectable crepe—but it was a breakthrough moment for me. I realized two things: One, the most basic combination of ingredients can create a most delectable treat. And two, if sweets can bring this much joy to someone's life, I want to be a part of it. The trouble was, eating sweets until I got a bellyache wouldn't pay my student loans. Plus, I still loved art and I was well aware of the difficulties in switching my career path. I wasn't ready to throw in that turpentine-stained towel just yet. So, with a design degree and plenty of ambition, I set out to find a job as a graphic designer. For a year I designed at a highly regarded cosmetics company, but it turns out that I don't really care about skincare.

Feeling the urge to jump ship and start down the culinary road, I hastily decided to enroll in pastry school. But days before I was to begin my formal training as a pastry student, the most amazing opportunity presented itself: a graphic designer gig at *Food & Wine* magazine. I had hit the jackpot, being able to parlay my love of baking into a design position, finally connecting my two passions. I could have my cake and eat it too. Literally.

Food & Wine isn't a workplace that cares about an outrageous pair of designer heels or the latest celebrity gossip. Unless of course that gossip involved the newest trend in guacamole or solving an age-old food debate: "What's better, sweet or savory breakfast?" or "How do you feel about cilantro?" Wars were started over such topics. *Food & Wine* culture thrives on these discussions, and who better to weigh in than the experts themselves? How inspiring, to be around folks who care about food as much as I do. My baking endeavors kicked into high gear. I was designing by day, baking by night, and sharing the fruits (or cakes) of my labor with my colleagues.

A few of them caught wind of my baking hijinks and asked me to make a celebration cake in the shape of a Converse sneaker. It was my first sculpted cake and my first time using fondant. (*Go big or go home, right?*) That cake was a success and I was hooked. One cake led to another and pretty soon I was the go-to cake-maker in our office. Baby showers, anniversaries, birthdays, you name it—I would schlep the cake from my East Village walk-up apartment to the subway and into our Midtown Manhattan office by 8 a.m. In hindsight, I should have petitioned to add "in-house baker" next to my "associate design director" title on the masthead. I found myself sleepwalking into our offices, exhausted from an all-nighter, with frosting plastered into my hair and bags under my eyes. But I wouldn't have it any other way. I was the luckiest amateur baker in the world, baking cakes for the likes of Dana Cowin and Gail Simmons. A nod of approval or positive feedback on anything I made meant the world to me.

It's not easy to hone your baking skills in a 4-by-4-foot kitchen while working full-time, but there's no crying in the kitchen. This is the path for so many people who pursue a second passion in life. Luckily I had some of the country's best taste-testers as colleagues and they were brutally honest. Their feedback was invaluable and I learned an endless amount through trial and error.

PASTRY CHOPS

Gaining confidence in the kitchen with no culinary training takes years. I think I speak for most self-taught bakers when I say we may never feel the confidence of a seasoned pastry chef, but with time and experience, we can certainly achieve the same results. My "culinary confidence" was only realized after endless mistakes were made and lessons learned. Let's not sugar-coat it here. I've made, like, a *ton* of mistakes. I've over-beaten my whipped cream to the point of butter, burned batches of cookies and scalded milk while attempting to make a pastry cream. Alas! Making mistakes is truly how you—and I—learn. That and picking up numerous tricks along the way from the magnificent cooks in my life.

Coming from a family of seven eaters and too many extended family members to count has given me access to some of the best home cooking around. Mothers, fathers, brothers, sisters and aunts hear this: Passing the love of food from one generation to the next is the best gift you can give.

My mother will never admit to being a great cook, but she certainly taught me the way around a kitchen. Moreover she allowed me to discover my own path in the food world, which wasn't always a pretty one. When I was growing up, my mother had a delicious hot dinner on the table every single night of the week. After a long day with five kids, she had zero desire to spend another minute in the kitchen whipping up a dessert. Passing the sweet-tooth duties on to me, my mother would graciously step out of the kitchen, fully knowing that she'd return to a mess. Many nights it looked as though a flour bomb had gone off in the kitchen, which was caked on with bits of butter and vanilla. I didn't realize until my adult years (when I had no one to clean up after me) that my mother knew it was all about the creativity—the experience of mixing ingredients and experimenting with recipes—not the final product. In granting me access to the kitchen and allowing chaos to ensue, she helped me grow into the creative person I am today. (*She also let me eat raw cookie dough in abundance and lick the bowl, and I intend to do the same for my son, nieces and nephews.*)

My unfiltered imagination would ultimately propel my decision to attend art school and become a designer, but there's no denying the connection between artists and bakers. The technical eye of a painter makes for an artful baker. Composition, color and form all play an important role in baking an edible masterpiece. My background has helped me tenfold as I pursue desserts. It's the backbone of this book.

As my design career in New York City continued, so grew my culinary confidence. And as more cakes were ordered, my style—and portfolio—began to evolve. With that came opportunity. Most were amazing—creating cakes for incredibly luxe events—but a couple were complete fails. (*There was an extremely humbling appearance on a Food Network Challenge. And although that was several years ago, it's still too soon to talk about it.*) My pride was restored when I was approached by Macy's to participate in their Annual Flower Show, held at the flagship store in New York's Herald Square. I was charged with designing and executing several cakes based on fairy tales to be showcased in their windows. With dozens of sketches, pounds of fondant, even a motorized windmill element, my most ambitious project yet was a huge success. Macy's was thrilled and the feedback was overwhelmingly positive. The success didn't register until my sister trekked up from Baltimore, saw my work in the windows facing Broadway, and began to cry. Granted, she cries during the Star Spangled Banner at baseball games, but her emotional response to my hard work was all the reassurance I needed. I had the chops to make it in the pastry world.

In the late summer of 2010, I joined the blogging community, launching Pixel Whisk (pixel-whisk.com). While I consider myself to be a slow blogger, meaning I post rather infrequently, my posts feature unique, thoughtful and original content. (*It's about quality, not quantity, right?*) In the beginning, my only purpose in creating Pixel Whisk was to share my dessert recipes and illustrate those recipes with detailed how-tos. But Pixel Whisk became more than just a recipe archive. It's provided me with a platform to share crowd-pleasing and artfully inspired dishes, D.I.Y. projects and entertaining tips. It's my real-life experiences—my mistakes *and* my baking triumphs. And now I'm lucky enough to share my delectable treats with you in this shiny little book.

Thanks for taking a bite,

ENTERTAINING TIPS I LEARNED FROM MY MOTHER:

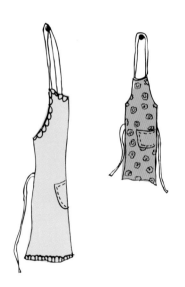

WHEN LIFE GIVES YOU LEMONS . . .
If your cake looks like it got run over by an 18-wheeler, that's OK. Ugly cake happens to the best of us, fear not. Cut the cake in the kitchen and serve everyone individual slices. They'll be excited to have a slice handed right to them, and you get to avoid the formal cake cutting charades.

ALWAYS SERVE CONDIMENTS IN CUTE DISHES.
No one wants to see the plastic container of mustard or sour cream. Gussy them up a bit by serving them in ramekins. My mother has about 3,000 if you need to borrow a few.

STOCK YOUR TABLE WITH PLENTY OF SNACKS.
What my family calls "the spread"—for when your guests arrive. If your guests say they aren't hungry, they're probably lying. Watch as they graze on the assortment of cheeses, veggies and dips you've so thoughtfully laid out.

WASTE NOTHING.
Extra pie dough can be sprinkled with cinnamon and sugar, rolled up and sliced into rounds called "pinwheels." Bake for 10 minutes at 350°F. Your kitchen will smell delicious and guests will have a tasty treat to snack on.

WHEN HOSTING, DRINK ONLY IN MODERATION.
Entertaining is a task that needs your undivided attention. One drink too many, and things can go downhill very quickly.

Making Christmas cookies with my siblings

Adding detail to the "windmill" cake for Macy's

My sister and I using leftover pie dough to make pinwheels

"Princess and the Pea" cake displayed in the Macy's windows

Tips & Tricks

ALL MEASURING CUPS ARE NOT EQUAL
Don't even think about measuring flour in that glass liquid measuring cup. Dry ingredients, including flour, should be spooned into the measuring cup, then leveled with an offset spatula. Liquid should only be measured in a liquid measuring cup with a spout. Unless it's brown sugar, don't pack ingredients into the measuring cup.

BAKING SODA IS NOT EQUAL TO BAKING POWDER
While both leaven your cakes and pastries by releasing gasses, baking soda is only activated when it comes in contact with an acid, such as milk or sour cream. Baking powder, however, is activated when exposed to moisture and heat. It starts to work once you mix the batter, then reacts again when baking in the oven. So don't swap one for the other, they aren't the same. You can make your own baking powder by mixing 1 teaspoon of baking soda with 2 teaspoons of cream of tartar.

CLEAN WHILE YOU COOK
This one was a necessity back when I had my 4-by-4-foot kitchen. Since I only had a 12-inch workspace—and didn't have a dishwasher—I constantly had to clean while baking. Even if you have a regular-size kitchen, nothing is worse than having a sink overflowing with dishes when all you really want to do is indulge in whatever you've just baked. Plus, keeping a clean kitchen means less bitching from your significant other.

CHOCOLATE IS DELICATE, TREAT HER WITH CARE
Even the tiniest drop of water will turn your chocolate into a granulated mess. And overheating your chocolate can lead to total devastation. Crying over a burned batch of chocolate isn't a good look for anyone. The trick to melting chocolate, without using a double boiler, is to microwave it slowly: Microwave it in a heat-safe bowl for 20 seconds, then stir. Microwave for another 20 seconds, then stir. Do this until there are just a few lumps left, then stir to melt the remaining lumps.

IT'S NOT A FRAT PARTY, DON'T CROWD THE OVEN
Pans should never touch each other or the sides of the oven. You'll end up with burned edges and unevenly baked goods.

KEEP YOUR DAIRY COMFORTABLE
Eggs, milk and butter should always be at room temperature. (Unless you're making a pie crust, in which case you want your butter very chilly.) Room-temperature ingredients emulsify better, creating a smooth batter. If you're in a rush, cube your butter, then pop it in the microwave for a few seconds to soften.

JUST BEAT IT
In a recipe, when I say, "beat the butter and sugar until light and fluffy," I mean it. Like, really beat it. For at least two minutes. The butter-sugar mixture should be a pale yellow color with a creamy texture. This creates air bubbles and a lighter texture in your final product.

KNOW THE BASICS
You don't need to be an expert, just have a few simple, go-to recipes, and everything else falls into place. If you have a great vanilla cake recipe, you can turn that into dozens of recipes: cinnamon apple cake, strawberry cupcakes, a layer cake and more. Knowing what flavors complement each other and having a solid foundation of the basic techniques are half the battle. Once you've established a baking foundation, you can focus on the details that make an impressive dessert.

MISE EN PLACE
This is a fancy way of saying, "Get your sh*t together, man!" It's so important to have all your ingredients in place before you begin. Nothing is worse than starting a cake only to realize you're out of eggs. Make a checklist of all your ingredients—and make sure nothing has expired.

NEVER MAKE YOUR OWN WEDDING CAKE
This may seem like a random tip, but I'm telling you not to bite off more than you can chew based on my own wedding-cake-making experience. If you happen to be getting hitched, and in the processes of planning you've convinced yourself that you can do it all, you can't. Unless your wedding involves a drive-thru ceremony on the Vegas strip followed by a pit stop at In-N-Out Burger, I advise against making your own tiered cake. You should be a relaxed, well-rested bride or groom. And if you make your own cake, you will likely be up all night before your wedding. I barely made it to the ceremony on time, fretting over the cake details until the very last minute. I literally walked down the aisle with chocolate frosting on my hands. Trust me, this is the one cake worth outsourcing to a pro.

INGREDIENTS MATTER

It should go without saying, but just in case: Desserts taste better when you use good ingredients. Here are a few pointers to keep in mind when shopping for ingredients.

Don't swap out sugar for a fake sugar substitute. It's not the same. Same goes for vanilla extract, use the pure stuff, not imitation vanilla.

Although it might cost a bit more, using high-end chocolate and cocoa powder is worth it. Higher quality chocolate adds depth and complexity to your desserts. (*Depth and complexity? Wow. Chocolate, you're perfect...will you marry me?*)

White chocolate can be deceiving. Always check the packaging to make sure cocoa butter is listed in the ingredients. Impostor white chocolate replaces that delicious cocoa butter with sugar and oils. When in doubt, go for a bar of white chocolate instead of the chips.

Don't use margarine, only full-fat unsalted butter. The good stuff. None of these recipes are fat-free. (*If you're looking for a juice cleanse, put down this book and walk away.*)

There's a reason why buttermilk is so prevalent in my cake recipes. It's deliciously tangy and contributes to a softer cake texture. It's also acidic, so it plays a role in the leavening process. If you find yourself in the middle of a recipe and in desperate need of buttermilk (*which should never happen if you read my earlier tips. See: Mise En Place*) you can make it. Just add one tablespoon of lemon juice or white vinegar to one cup of whole milk. Stir, then let stand at room temperature for about ten minutes before using.

the Hardware

assume that when it comes to the hardware, you already have the essentials: baking pans, whisks, mixing bowls, etc. The tools listed here are the other things I simply cannot live without, and I suggest you use them, too. In fact, most of the recipes in this book use at least a couple of these tools. The majority of these items can be found at craft stores in the baking aisle. But keep your eyes peeled, as you may strike gold in the unlikeliest of places. I often find supplies at my shopping mecca, HomeGoods. If you still have trouble finding these essentials in a store, just order them online.

ALPHABET COOKIE CUTTERS
A necessity if you've ever wanted to write a random edible note. (*And who doesn't?*)

CAKE BOARDS
You can get by with the cheap basic corrugated cardboard ones for most projects. If you're making a fancy wedding cake, then I'd buy the more substantial ones that won't buckle. Cake boards come in varied sizes and are a necessity when building a tiered cake. You want the board to be the exact size as your cake tier. Once you frost the cake the board will be hidden, and you'll still be able to move the cake easily.

CAKE TURNTABLE
Using a cake turntable will make you feel like a pro. It rotates the cake, helping you apply an even coat of frosting like no one's business. The moment you start using one, you'll start making better cakes. Seriously.

CIRCLE COOKIE CUTTERS
Every baker should own a set of round stainless-steel cutters that vary from 1 inch to 4½ inches in diameter. You will use them for anything from cutting fondant circles to making homemade biscuits. Wipe them clean after use and never let these babies go.

EDIBLE-INK MARKERS
These are a godsend when you need to create a small detail on a cake. They are completely nontoxic and much easier to control than a tiny paintbrush and a shaky hand after three cups of coffee. I use AmeriColor Gourmet Writers, which come in a pack with 10 assorted colors.

FONDANT SMOOTHER
The fondant smoother is to cakes what the steamer is to a wrinkled dress. This plastic paddle is the best way to smooth out any lumps in the fondant, leaving you with a perfect "blank canvas."

GEL FOOD COLORING
Found at any baking supply and most craft stores, gel food coloring is the best way to color your frostings and fondant. The gel consistency ads vibrant color without the extra water found in traditional food coloring. I use AmeriColor brand and I highly recommend their electric green color for any time you need a leaf- or grass-colored frosting.

KITCHEN SCISSORS

I swear by kitchen scissors for all-purpose use in the kitchen. Get a real pair of kitchen shears that you can wash. Use them for anything from creating small pieces of fondant to cutting slices of pizza. If you eat as much pizza as my household does, you might require two pairs of scissors.

LUSTER DUST

Although it comes in dozens of assorted colors, gold and silver luster dust are generally all you need. Mix a small amount in a little vodka, and use a paintbrush to decorate with the luster dust. It is an incredible way to finish fondant cakes, molded chocolate or fancy cookies. And it's completely edible! Find it at the occasional craft store, online and at all cake supply stores.

MASON JARS

Mason jars are the solution for anything from canning preserves to storing ingredients, even baking a pie in a jar. They are adorable, have an airtight seal and many are ovenproof. Also, mason jars serve as the perfect vessel for any cocktail. What's not to like?!

MERINGUE POWDER

Meringue powder is a substitute for egg whites, used in frostings and meringues. Sure, you can use raw egg whites to create royal icing, but I prefer meringue powder for its simplicity. Meringue powder is, in fact, made from eggs, so it's all good. It's faster, less messy and still has the stability and texture of a traditional royal icing. You can find it in the baking aisle of any craft store.

MICROPLANE

The microplane is the only tool that can give you perfect zest from citrus. There's really no other way around it. Just get one, they're cheap. Plus, they also are great for making finely grated cheese. Yes!

OFFSET SPATULA

An offset spatula is not like any old spatula. It has a flexible stainless steel blade and is angled so you can frost a cake to perfection. It's also great for smoothing out batters and removing cookies from the pan. This is a miracle tool and I recommend having several small ones and a couple larger ones, too.

OVEN THERMOMETER

Not every oven is calibrated to have the most accurate temperature. In fact, my decade-old oven is straight up moody at times and her temperature can fluctuate quite a bit. Even though it says it's 350°F, the temperature can actually be 400°F. It's important to keep an eye on the cooking times as things can burn if your oven runs hot. An oven thermometer lets you adjust the settings to account for those fluctuations. This handy tool costs only a few bucks, making it a no-brainer for any baker.

PADDLE-SPATULA ATTACHMENT

With this stand mixer attachment, wiping down the sides of your bowl is a thing of the past. This paddle-spatula hybrid replaces the traditional paddle attachment for your stand mixer. Several companies sell them, and they're all pretty much the same—a time-saving, bowl-scraping, "Why didn't I have this before?" life-saver.

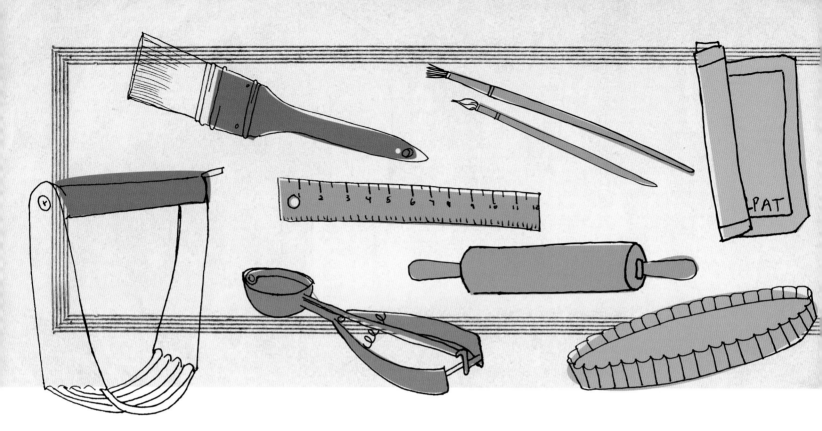

PAINT BRUSHES
Keep a clean set for kitchen business only. These are the best way to apply colorful details to cakes and cookies. Go ahead, unleash your inner artist.

PASTRY BLENDER
This is the one-and-only tool to create flawless pie dough every time. It's a simple thing, just a handle with a few blades attached. But the blades cut the butter into the flour, creating the perfect ratio of fat to flour.

PASTRY BRUSH
Brushes are great for applying melted butter or an egg wash to pies before baking. They also come in handy when you need to clean crumbs off a finished cake.

PIPING BAGS AND TIPS
Piping bags come in different sizes and materials. I like the 14-inch disposable plastic piping bags, which come in boxes of fifty. They're easy to maneuver and create a consistent flow of frosting. You can get a

small starter set of piping tips with couplers (they help the tip attach to the piping bag) at any craft store. In this book, all the royal icing piping can be done with a size 3 round piping tip. If you're really in a pinch, a re-sealable plastic bag with the corner snipped off works, too. As with most aspects of baking, practice makes perfect. Lucky for us, even piping mistakes still taste good.

RIMMED SHEET PAN
These are great for baking anything from cookies to a sheet cake. Purchase at least two 12-by-18-inch pans with a 1-inch rim.

ROLLING PIN
When I would make Christmas cookies as a kid, my mom would give me an old can of soup to use as a rolling pin. Although I applaud her resourcefulness, I don't recommend it. Get a sturdy wooden rolling pin. It will keep your fondant or dough at an even thickness.

RULER
When I started art school I got a traditional, no-frills, red toolbox. In the toolbox was a stainless steel 15" ruler. I still have it and it is one of the most used kitchen tools I have. Aside from making templates and measuring fondant, the ruler comes in handy to measure baking sheets and cookie cutters.

SILICONE BAKING LINERS
These liners make the most perfect nonstick surface for baking. They're a reusable alternative to parchment paper and eliminate any burned cookie edges you may have struggled with in the past. I prefer Silpat, available online or at any store that sells baking supplies. They're also a great work surface for rolling out fondant or working with anything sticky.

SIFTER
Call me old fashioned, but sifters are by far the most fun kitchen tool to use. They break up any clumps in your flour or cocoa powder and they're perfect for incorporating all your dry ingredients. Many people

skip the step of sifting their dry ingredients, but it really does make a difference in the texture of your baked goods. Sifters are also great for dusting flour on your work surface before rolling out pie dough, or finishing a dessert with confectioners' sugar.

SPRING-RELEASE ICE CREAM SCOOP

Any old ice cream scoop just won't do the trick when it comes to evenly dividing batters and cookie dough. It must be a scoop with the spring-release feature. I prefer two sizes, the 2-inch scoop to pour cake batter into cupcake liners, and the 1¼-inch for scooping cookie dough.

STAND MIXER

There are two types of people in the world: The ones who display their stand mixer out on the kitchen counter, and those who keep it tucked away in a cabinet. Back in the days when I literally had 12 inches of counter space, my stand mixer was still proudly on display—a baker's badge of honor. The classic KitchenAid mixer really is the only way to

go. If you don't have one it's probably because you aren't married yet, as a mixer seems to top every wedding registry. Personally, I didn't have the patience to wait for an engagement or registry. Instead, I asked for a stand mixer for Christmas when I was in high school. I still use the same one almost daily. And like a marriage, you and your stand mixer will be together for a very long time, so make sure you pick a color you like.

TART PAN

You probably already have a pie plate, and that's just fine—if you want to be average. Don't get me wrong, I love all pies—sweet, savory, rustic, or refined. I just think tart pans yield a fancier dessert. A 9- or 10-inch tart pan should do the trick.

TURBINADO SUGAR

Also called Sugar In The Raw, this coarse crystalized sugar is perfect for finishing desserts like pies, muffins and shortbread cookies. Aside from having a faint molasses flavor, turbinado sugar adds a welcome little crunch to your baked treats.

VODKA

Baking can get stressful. Take a shot of vodka and within a minute, you should feel more relaxed. (*Kidding. Sort of.*) Actually, vodka can be a very useful tool when decorating cakes. Use a small amount mixed with luster dust or gel food coloring and apply with a paintbrush. Unlike water (which will make your fondant sticky and soggy) the alcohol in vodka evaporates, leaving a beautiful finish. It also works to dilute food coloring.

Make a Statement

When you head out to the office in the morning or prep for a first date, you likely take a moment to decide what you are going to wear. You put at least a little consideration into how you present yourself. (*Unless, like me, you've discovered jeggings, in which case you'll probably never wear real pants again.*) Those of you who like to make an impression with your wardrobe probably care about how you entertain, as well. If you dress to impress with a pair of shoes or a blazer, shouldn't you also make a statement with the desserts you serve? You have a ton of personality—your food should, too. These recipes are the perfect way to make a statement without spending hours in the kitchen. They're boldly stylish, eye-catching, and most importantly, delicious. The Monogram Cookies, for example, allow you to personalize in bold black and white. The Rocky Road Cookies recipe is as simple as recipes come, but the giant marshmallow circle in the middle of the cookie will no doubt impress. These are the tried and true desserts we all love, just with a little more personality.

"SUNNY SIDE UP" MERINGUES

BLACK & WHITE MONOGRAM COOKIES

OMBRÉ POLKA DOT CAKE

STRAWBERRY SHORTBREAD STACKS

ROCKY ROAD COOKIES

EARL GREY TEA CAKES

FAUX TACOS

"SUNNY SIDE UP" MERINGUES

I love it when desserts have a sense of humor. It's especially gratifying when guests think I'm serving one thing when in fact it's a completely different dish. You'll see a few trick desserts pop up in this book as they are truly my favorite. (See the Faux Tacos on pg. 43 and the Tree Ring Spice Cookies on pg. 91.) These meringues mimic sunny side up eggs but are certainly best served as a dessert. (*Of course I'll never judge someone who eats sweets for breakfast. A pancake is really just cake, isn't it?*) The best thing about this sweet-and-tart recipe is the yin and yang of the meringue and the curd. They pair together so very well and yet are complete opposites. While meringue uses only egg whites, the lemon curd gladly accepts those rejected yolks. Not to take sides here, but I'm on Team Curd, as I absolutely love those vibrant yellow "yolks."

TIP
Straining the lemon curd is a must. If you don't, you risk having little "scrambled egg" bits in the curd.

Makes 12 cookies

MERINGUE COOKIES
3 egg whites
¾ cup granulated sugar
pinch of salt

Preheat oven to 200°F. Line two baking sheets with baking liners or parchment paper.

Place egg whites in the bowl of a stand mixer fitted with the whisk attachment. Beat on high speed until white and foamy. Slowly pour the sugar into the bowl, mixing on high speed until stiff peaks form, then add the salt.

Use a spoon to evenly space 6 portions of the meringue onto each parchment or lined cookie sheet. With the back of the spoon, spread the meringue to make flat disks about 3 inches wide. Dip your fingertip in water and lightly tap down any peaks.

Bake meringues for about 1 hour and 45 minutes, or until dry. Set aside to cool.

LEMON CURD
4 egg yolks
½ cup granulated sugar
Zest of 1 lemon
½ cup fresh lemon juice
6 tablespoons unsalted butter, cubed

In a saucepan set over medium-low heat, combine the egg yolks and sugar and whisk until incorporated.

Add in the lemon zest and juice, stirring constantly until thickened, or about 8 minutes.

Strain the mixture into a clean bowl. Then stir in the cubes of butter until completely melted.

Cool to room temperature, stirring occasionally to prevent a skin from forming on the top. Then cover the bowl tightly with plastic wrap and refrigerate until chilled.

To Assemble:
When both cookies and lemon curd are cool, spoon a heaping teaspoon of curd on top of each cookie.

Unassembled meringue cookies will keep for about a week in an airtight container. Assembled meringues should be eaten that day. Store any leftover curd in the refrigerator for up to a week.

Monograms are having quite the moment right now. Let's embrace this typographic—albeit, slightly preppy—movement with these two-color cookies. They're the perfect takeaway for a wedding, shower, birthday, you-name-it celebration. The cookies themselves are extra-special with a hint of cardamom and honey, and the royal icing gives you the chance to personalize, then dries hard for a nice sweet crunch.

BLACK & WHITE MONOGRAM COOKIES

Makes 2 dozen cookies

CARDAMOM-HONEY COOKIES

2 cups all-purpose flour, plus more for dusting

½ teaspoon ground cardamom

¼ teaspoon salt

½ teaspoon baking soda

½ cup (1 stick) unsalted butter, softened

⅓ cup granulated sugar

¼ cup honey

1 egg

1 teaspoon vanilla extract

In a bowl, whisk or sift together the flour, cardamom, salt and baking soda, then set aside.

In another bowl, use a stand mixer fitted with the paddle attachment to beat the butter and sugar on medium speed until light and fluffy.

Add the honey, egg and vanilla. Continue mixing on medium speed until well blended, about 1 minute. Slowly add the flour mixture on low speed until the dough just comes together.

Scoop out the dough onto a sheet of plastic wrap and smooth into a flattened disk. Wrap tightly and refrigerate until chilled, at least 2 hours.

Preheat the oven to 350°F. Line two baking sheets with baking liners or parchment paper.

Working with your chilled disk, roll out the dough to ⅛-inch thick on a floured work surface. Use an inverted glass or 3-inch cookie cutter to cut out the cookies and place them 1 inch apart on the baking sheets. Don't be afraid to vary the shape of the cookie. As long as the monogram letter fits comfortably on top of the cookie, you could change the shape to a diamond or square. Gather and re-roll scraps to make more cookies.

Bake for 8 to 10 minutes or until the edges turn golden brown. Cool completely before icing.

ROYAL ICING

4 cups (about 1 lb.) confectioners' sugar

3 tablespoons meringue powder

½ cup water

1 teaspoon vanilla extract

Black gel food coloring

Alphabet Template (pg. 156)

In the bowl of a stand mixer fitted with the whisk attachment, beat the first four ingredients together until icing is shiny and soft peaks form. The consistency is right when you remove the whisk attachment and the peak falls onto itself. If icing is too thick, add more water, 1 teaspoon at a time. Spoon half of the white icing into a bowl and set aside.

Add several drops of black food coloring to the icing remaining in the mixer and beat until the icing is the desired shade of black. The icing will darken as it sits; if it looks dark gray at this point, know it will dry darker. Spoon half of the black icing into a piping bag fitted with a size 3 tip. Spoon the remaining half into a shallow dish for dipping the cookies.

Repeat the above steps with the white icing and you will have piping bags and shallow dishes of both the black and white icing.

Carefully dip the tops of half of the cookies into the white icing, then place them on a sheet of parchment paper or a cooling rack. Repeat with the remaining cookies in the black icing, then set aside and allow the icing to harden.

Tape a sheet of parchment paper over the Alphabet Template (pg. 156) and pipe your desired letters in black and white. Pipe the outline of the letter first, then fill in the inside. (Make extras, just in case any break.) Let the icing harden completely, then carefully remove the letter from the parchment.

To Assemble:
When both the frosted cookies and icing letters have hardened, use a scant amount of icing to affix a letter to each cookie. Store cookies in an airtight container in a cool, dry place for up to a week.

TIP

Keep the bowl of icing covered with a damp paper towel as you work. It will dry out as fast as it takes you to eat one of these cookies.

Get creative with the icing! Pipe dots or a zigzag border around the edge of the cookie.

OMBRÉ POLKA DOT CAKE

When it comes to making a cake that will impress without hours of labor on your part, here's the winner. This cake is incredibly stylish, thanks to its ombré exterior. (*You can achieve an ombré with any color, so if blue isn't your thing, pick a color that suits you.*) Don't be intimidated by fondant, this is the perfect intro if you've never worked with it before.

If the impressive ombré coloring doesn't win your friends over, the delicious Buttermilk Vanilla Cake and Cream Cheese Buttercream are sure to do the trick.

Makes one 8-inch layer cake

BUTTERMILK VANILLA CAKE

2 ¾ cups all-purpose flour
1 tablespoon baking powder
1 teaspoon salt
1 cup (2 sticks) unsalted butter, softened
2 cups granulated sugar
5 eggs
2 teaspoons vanilla extract
1½ cups buttermilk

Preheat the oven to 350°F. Grease three 8-inch round cake pans, line the bottoms with parchment paper, grease and set aside.

In a medium bowl, sift or whisk together the flour, baking powder and salt, and set aside.

Beat the butter and sugar together in the bowl of a stand mixer fitted with the paddle attachment until light and fluffy. Add the eggs, one at a time, until incorporated. Scrape down the sides of the bowl and add the vanilla.

With the mixer on low, add the flour mixture, alternating with the buttermilk until the batter is completely mixed and smooth.

Divide the batter evenly among cake pans and bake for 40 minutes or until a toothpick inserted in the center of a cake comes out clean. Cool completely.

crumb coat

CREATING A CRUMB COAT

is an essential step to a smooth finished cake. It's a very thin layer of frosting on the cake that keeps those little crumbs stuck on the cake and out of your frosting. If you're covering a cake in fondant, a crumb coat is a smooth surface for the fondant to stick to.

First, make sure all the cake layers are even and trim any protruding pieces. Then use an offset spatula to spread an even layer all over the cake. Chill the cake in the fridge for 30 minutes before you apply the final frosting layer or fondant.

CREAM CHEESE BUTTERCREAM

¾ cup (1½ sticks) unsalted butter, softened
4 ounces (½ package) cream cheese, softened
4 cups (about 1 lb.) confectioners' sugar
1 teaspoon vanilla extract
Pinch of salt
Blue gel food coloring

In the bowl of a stand mixer fitted with the paddle attachment, cream the butter and cream cheese until well combined.

Slowly add the confectioners' sugar and mix until frosting is creamy and smooth. Mix in the vanilla and salt. If the frosting is too thick, mix in a teaspoon or two of milk.

Add a few drops of blue food coloring and mix until you have the desired shade.

TIP

Make sure the cream cheese and butter are both at room temperature, otherwise they won't mix properly and you'll have streaks of cream cheese.

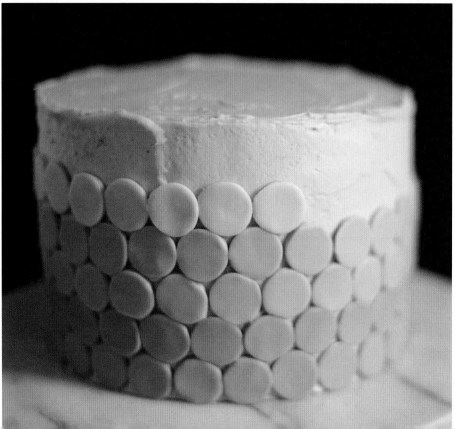

OMBRÉ FONDANT DOTS

You'll Need:

1 lb. package of ready-to-use white rolled fondant

Blue gel food coloring

¾-inch round cutter

Confectioners' sugar and cornstarch, for dusting

Prepare a clean, nonstick workspace to color and cut your fondant.

Separate the white fondant into 4 equal pieces. Starting with the darkest color, tint one of the fondant pieces with a few drops of food coloring. Knead the fondant until the color is fully integrated and there are no streaks. To make the color richer, add more food coloring. Wrap tightly in plastic wrap and set aside.

Take another piece of white fondant and add fewer drops of food coloring to tint it a slightly lighter shade. Wrap and set aside.

Repeat with the last two fondant pieces, coloring each one a lighter shade, until you have four gradient shades. If the color of your fondant doesn't look vibrant enough, let it sit for a few hours to absorb the color. It will become darker as it rests.

TIP

Fondant dries out quickly, so make sure anything you aren't using is wrapped tightly in plastic wrap.

Use a sharp serrated knife to slice each cake into two even layers. This will create 6 thin cake layers and will look more impressive when you cut into the cake.

Place the first layer on your cake stand and use an offset spatula to frost the top of the layer.

Place the second layer of this cake on top and frost the top, continuing to stack and add frosting between each layer. You'll use half of the frosting to fill the cake layers and the other half to create a thin crumb coat (see pg. 33) covering the outside of the cake. Place the cake in the refrigerator to chill until you're ready to decorate.

Lightly dust your workspace with a 50/50 mix of confectioners' sugar and cornstarch.

Working with one piece at a time, unwrap and roll out the fondant to about ⅛-inch thick. Use the ¾-inch round cutter to cut as many circles as you can from each of the four fondant sections.

Remove cake from fridge. Starting from the bottom of the cake, place the darkest shade of dots closely together in a single row all around the cake, pressing lightly so the dot sticks to the buttercream.

Make 2 complete layers of the darkest shade, then switch to the second-darkest shade. Continue placing the dots in rows, until you cover the entire cake from bottom to top.

Store covered cake in the refrigerator for up to 3 days.

Is there anyone who doesn't love strawberries and cream? Although there are a million ways to combine the two, this recipe in particular really lets the ingredients shine—and the stacked presentation makes this dessert effortlessly fabulous. Make these stacks in the summer, when fresh strawberries are abundant and extra-sweet. Oh, and keep this shortbread recipe in the arsenal for when you need a dessert in a pinch. It's extremely versatile and couldn't be easier.

STRAWBERRY SHORTBREAD STACKS

Makes 2 dozen cookies

SHORTBREAD COOKIES

1 cup (2 sticks) unsalted butter, softened

1 cup confectioners' sugar

1 vanilla bean, split lengthwise, seeds scraped, or
1 ½ teaspoons vanilla extract

2 cups all-purpose flour

¾ teaspoon salt

¼ cup of milk

½ cup turbinado sugar

Beat the butter in a stand mixer fitted with the paddle attachment until smooth and pale yellow.

Turn the mixer on low, then slowly add in the confectioners' sugar, mixing until incorporated. Add in the vanilla bean seeds, flour and salt and mix until just blended.

Gather the dough onto a sheet of plastic wrap, form into a flat disk, wrap tightly and refrigerate for at least 2 hours.

Preheat oven to 350°F and line two baking sheets with parchment paper. Pour the milk into a shallow bowl, pour the turbinado sugar into a dish, and set both aside.

Lightly flour a clean workspace and remove the chilled dough from the fridge. Roll dough until it's about ⅛-inch thick. Use a 3-inch round cutter (or cookie cutter of choice) and cut out several cookies. Gather scraps together and re-chill dough if necessary before rolling out for more circles.

Dip half of the cookie into the milk, then dredge the dipped half in the sugar so half of the cookie is sugar-coated. Place cookies 1 inch apart on the baking sheet and bake for 10 to12 minutes or until edges just begin to turn golden. Set aside to cool.

STRAWBERRY WHIPPED CREAM

1 lb. fresh strawberries, hulled and sliced thin

1 tablespoon granulated sugar

1 pint (16 ounces) cold heavy whipping cream

¼ cup confectioners' sugar

Macerate the strawberries by tossing them with the granulated sugar in a bowl. Set aside for about an hour so the juices thicken and the strawberries soften.

Make the whipped cream by beating the cream and confectioners' sugar in the bowl of a stand mixer fitted with the whisk attachment. Start on medium so the cream doesn't splatter, then increase the speed to high once the mixture starts to thicken. Beat until stiff peaks form.

Carefully fold in the strawberries and refrigerate until you're ready to assemble the shortbread stacks.

To Assemble:
Sandwich a spoonful of the strawberry whipped cream between two shortbread cookies and stack to your heart's content.

TIP

Using quality ingredients really makes a difference. The fewer the ingredients in a recipe, the more important it is to have the high-quality stuff. Go for a rich heavy cream and a full-fat unsalted butter.

Save time! Bake the cookies and macerate the strawberries the day before.

ROCKY ROAD COOKIES

Everyone needs a go-to cookie recipe—the thing you whip up when you need a dessert in, like, 15 minutes. These Rocky Road Cookies are my go-to, and they're simply amazing. They're rich, gooey and decadent, like a chocolate fudge brownie, but they require only a fraction of the baking time. Oh, and did I mention they're flourless? Go ahead and win over those friends of yours who are gluten-free.

Makes 12 cookies

2½ cups confectioners' sugar
1 cup unsweetened cocoa powder
¼ teaspoon salt
1 teaspoon instant espresso powder
3 egg whites (slightly less than ½ cup)
1 teaspoon vanilla extract
¾ cup semisweet chocolate chips
¾ cup chopped walnuts
6 large marshmallows, cut in half with kitchen scissors

Preheat the oven to 350°F. Line two baking sheets with liners or parchment paper.

In a large bowl, whisk or sift together the confectioners' sugar, cocoa, salt and espresso powder.

Mix in the egg whites and vanilla until smooth and no lumps remain. Add the chocolate chips and walnuts, stirring until fully incorporated and dough is gooey.

Use a cookie scoop to drop round balls of dough on the baking sheets. Leave about 2 inches between cookies. Press a marshmallow half firmly into the top of each dough ball.

Bake the cookies for 10 to 12 minutes, or until the marshmallows are nice and toasty on top. The cookies will look shiny and cracked. Cool slightly before eating.

TIP
Don't forget the espresso powder. Remember, chocolate baked goods always taste better with a hint of espresso!

Swap out the walnuts for any nut you prefer, or add graham cracker pieces for a new take on s'mores.

Earl Grey is fragrant
and pairs perfectly
with the Lavender-
Lemon Glaze, but you
can experiment with
different types of tea.

EARL GREY TEA CAKES

Whether it's salt and pepper, PB & J, Laverne and Shirley, or a girl and her cupcake, you don't mess with a good pair. Earl Grey tea and lavender, they're made for one another, too. These cupcakes are the perfect example of how easy infusing flavors into cake can be. The trick is to steep the tea in the milk before adding it to the dry ingredients. In staying true to the simplicity of a cup of tea, I opted for a light glaze instead of a heavy buttercream frosting. The result is a delicious Earl Grey cupcake with a tart and fragrant lavender-lemon glaze. Your teatime just got a heck of a lot better.

Makes 12 cupcakes

EARL GREY CUPCAKES

⅔ cup milk
4 teaspoons Earl Grey loose leaf tea or 4 teabags
1½ cups all-purpose flour
1½ teaspoons baking powder
½ teaspoon salt
½ cup (1 stick) butter, softened
1 cup granulated sugar
2 eggs
1 teaspoon vanilla extract

Preheat the oven to 350°F and line a standard muffin tin with 12 cupcake liners.

In a microwave-safe liquid measuring cup, heat the milk and Earl Grey tea for 1 minute. Let the tea steep for at least 10 minutes. (The longer it steeps, the stronger the flavor will be in your cupcakes.)

Whisk together the flour, baking powder and salt in a bowl and set aside.

Beat the butter and sugar until light and fluffy in the bowl of a stand mixer fitted with the paddle attachment. Add the eggs, one at a time, beating until just incorporated, then add the vanilla.

Remove the teabags, or strain your steeped milk into a pourable cup.

Add the flour mixture, alternating with the tea-infused milk, until the batter is completely incorporated. Divide the batter into the muffin tin, filling each cup about ¾ full. If you have a small amount of extra batter, don't overfill the cups, just make more cupcakes!

Bake for 15 minutes or until a toothpick inserted in the center comes out clean. Set aside to cool.

LAVENDER-LEMON GLAZE

2 heaping teaspoons dried lavender buds
Juice of 1 lemon
¾ cup confectioners' sugar

Combine the lavender buds and lemon juice in a microwave-safe bowl. Heat for 35 seconds. (The juice will have a light-pink hue).

Strain the lavender buds, then add the confectioners' sugar to the lemon juice. Mix until the glaze is smooth and no lumps remain. If your glaze is too thin, add more sugar. If the glaze is too thick, add a few drops of water to thin it out.

To Assemble:
Peel the liners off and carefully drop the cupcakes into teacups. Spoon glaze onto each cupcake and garnish with a few lavender buds.

FAUX TACOS

When it comes to the savory realm, my favorite food, without a doubt, is tacos. Tacos are the one thing I could probably eat for every meal for the rest of my life. That is, as long as Choco Tacos were included—and a few of these humble little cookie tacos. Like my Sunny Side Up Meringues, these tacos will also make your guests do a double take. While they look like traditional savory tacos, they're actually a sweet and crunchy tuile cookie, filled with a rich chocolate crumble, coconut flakes and a drizzle of white chocolate.

YOU'LL NEED:
Tuile Taco Shells (see recipe)
Chocolate Crumble, for the meat filling (see recipe)
White Chocolate Ganache, for the sour cream (see recipe)
Tinted Coconut, for the lettuce and cheese (see recipe)
Hot Tamales candies, halved, for the tomatoes

Makes about 18 shells

TUILE TACO SHELLS
½ cup all-purpose flour
½ cup granulated sugar
¼ teaspoon salt
4 tablespoons (½ stick) unsalted butter, melted
3 egg whites
½ teaspoon vanilla extract

Combine the flour, sugar and salt in a large bowl with a whisk. Add melted butter, egg whites and vanilla, whisking until fully incorporated. Cover and set batter aside for about 45 minutes.

Preheat oven to 350°F and line a baking sheet with a liner or parchment paper.

Use a teaspoon to drop large spoonfuls of batter onto the baking sheet, leaving about 2 inches between scoops. Use the back of your spoon to spread the batter into 3-inch circles.

Bake for 10 to 12 minutes, or until edges turn golden brown.

Working quickly, make the taco shell by carefully draping the cookie over the rim of a large mixing bowl. If the cookies cool too quickly for you to mold them, pop them back in the oven for a minute to soften and try again.

Repeat with any remaining batter, until all the taco shells are baked, molded and cooled.

Any leftover Chocolate Crumble makes the perfect topping for ice cream.

CHOCOLATE CRUMBLE

1 cup all-purpose flour
1 cup light brown sugar
½ cup unsweetened cocoa powder
¼ teaspoon salt
½ cup (1 stick) unsalted butter, melted
½ teaspoon vanilla extract

Preheat your oven to 350°F and line a baking sheet with a liner or parchment paper.

Use a fork to mix the flour, brown sugar, cocoa, and salt together.

Drizzle the melted butter and vanilla over the mixture and stir until all the dry ingredients are evenly moistened and the mixture resembles potting soil.

Spread the crumble evenly onto prepared baking sheet and bake for 20 minutes, or until your kitchen smells like heaven. Cool completely and set aside.

Taco shells, chocolate crumble and tinted coconut can be made in advance and stored in airtight containers.

TIP

WHITE CHOCOLATE "SOUR CREAM"

½ cup white chocolate, chips or chopped
(the real stuff, not white candy melts)

Heat white chocolate in the microwave for 20 seconds, then stir, repeating until the chocolate is just about melted. Spoon into a zip top bag and place in a cup of warm water to keep the chocolate melted until assembly.

TINTED COCONUT "LETTUCE & CHEDDAR CHEESE"

1 cup of sweetened coconut flakes
Yellow food coloring
Green food coloring

Divide the coconut between two small bowls, one bowl with ¾ cup and another with ¼ cup.

Add two drops of green food coloring to bowl filled with ¾ cup of coconut and mix with a fork or clean hands to fully incorporate color into the coconut.

Add two drops of yellow food coloring to the other bowl and mix, adding more food coloring if needed.

To Assemble:
When ready to serve, first fill the taco shells with the "meat filling," and then layer on "Lettuce" and "Cheddar Cheese."

Remove white chocolate from water and snip off the corner of the zip top bag. Drizzle "sour cream" over the tacos and top with halved Hot Tamales.

Candy
Land

alk into any candy store and you'll likely experience a wave of nostalgic excitement. Maybe it's the fact that candy was a rare commodity when I was a kid—or perhaps it's recalling that sheer youthful sugar rush—but I rarely pass a decent candy store without making an impulse purchase. I fondly remember summers on Boston's South Shore as a kid, begging my mom to let me walk to Riddle's Convenience Store for a Ring Pop and a box of candy cigarettes. (*Can you believe they still sell those?*) There's a reason why the saying "a kid in a candy store" holds true: There's no better feeling than having unlimited options for tooth decay right at your fingertips. This chapter is devoted to candy and the amazing treats you can create with and inspired by it. That's right, Willy Wonka's got nothing on you.

Don't be intimidated by making your own caramel, it's actually really easy.

TIP

TAKE-A-BREAK BARS

If you ask me, the Take 5 bar is the king of all candy bars. In fact, I should get some sort of commission for the number of times I've converted a candy bar skeptic to the Take 5. Peanut butter, pretzels, caramel, peanuts and chocolate. Hallelujah! It really is that good. These Take-A-Break Bars are my homage to the beloved candy bar. They are the epitome of a successful salty-sweet treat and I suggest having them within an arm's reach whenever possible.

Makes 12 bars

3 heaping cups mini pretzels
1 cup peanut butter
1 cup, plus 2 tablespoons granulated sugar, divided
3 tablespoons water
½ cup heavy cream, at room temperature
½ teaspoon vanilla extract
¾ cup peanuts, coarsely chopped
1 heaping cup of high-quality semisweet chocolate chips
Sea salt flakes (such as Maldon), for topping

Preheat the oven to 350°F. Line an 8-inch square pan with parchment paper.

In a food processor, pulse the pretzels, peanut butter and 2 tablespoons of sugar until the pretzels are crushed and the mixture clumps together.

Press mixture firmly into the pan and bake for 10 minutes. Keep the oven preheated.

In a saucepan over medium heat, stir remaining cup of sugar and water until sugar dissolves.

Increase heat to high and boil sugar for about 5 minutes, or until the color begins to darken. Carefully pick up the saucepan and tilt to swirl caramelized sugar to mix and continue to cook for another minute, or until it's a medium-amber color.

Remove from the heat and carefully whisk in the heavy cream and vanilla. (It will bubble violently, so stir carefully!) Whisk until it stops bubbling, then set aside to cool.

Pour caramel over the pretzel crust, then evenly top with chopped peanuts. Cover the peanuts with the chocolate chips and bake for 10 minutes.

Remove the bars from the oven and use an offset spatula or knife to smooth out the chocolate while it's still warm.

Sprinkle sea salt flakes on top of the chocolate and let cool to room temperature.

Refrigerate for a couple hours, or until chocolate hardens. Slice into bars and serve!

The lighter the candy, the better. (*I don't mean diet candy. I mean lightweight; heavy candy won't stick to the cone as well as the icing dries.*)

TIP

CANDY TREES

Sorry folks, but the days of party decorating with rolls of crepe paper and a Mylar balloon are long gone. It's time to step up your entertaining game with a creative tablescape, and these candy trees are just the ticket. Candy trees are not only sweet and stunning, they add height to table decor. Basic Styrofoam cones get a coat of royal icing, and are then dressed up with colorful candy bling. It's a good day for those cones—and anyone who loves candy.

YOU'LL NEED:
Assorted colorful candies: I recommend Necco Wafers, candy corns, peppermints, Good N Plenty or crushed Lemon Drops
Royal Icing (see recipe)
White Styrofoam cones in varied sizes (available at craft stores)

ROYAL ICING
4 cups confectioners' sugar
3 tablespoons meringue powder
¼ cup water

Beat the ingredients together until icing is smooth and stiff peaks form. Cover the bowl of icing with a damp paper towel to prevent it from drying out.

Set aside until you're ready to assemble the candy trees.

To Assemble:
Working with one cone at a time, use an offset spatula to spread the icing over half of the cone.

Place the candies closely together, hiding as much of the cone as possible. Repeat with the remaining half of the cone, until the entire cone is covered. Once the cones dry they'll last for months.

COCONUT BLISS CAKE

I've had a longtime love affair with coconut candy. Almond Joys and Mounds bars are always the first to disappear from my Halloween stash. (*I use the present tense because at my age, I proudly continue to collect Halloween candy.*) This recipe is a deconstruction of the Almond Joy, reassembled in the best possible way. The coconut cake is inspired by my aunt Edna's incredibly light and flawless coconut cake. At 91, Edna is the eldest of my mother's 15 siblings (*Yes, 15!*), and her coconut cake is the thing dreams are made of. Her frosting is simple, made with fresh coconut, sugar and egg whites—but cracking into a coconut is no joke. While aunt Edna never seems to have trouble with coconuts, I've nearly lost fingers trying to pry one open. So to preserve our appendages, we'll just stick to store-bought coconut flakes for this recipe. One bite of this cake, coated in a decadent chocolate fudge sauce and adorned in almonds, and you'll be hooked. It's the Almond Joy, all grown up.

Makes one 8-inch layer cake

COCONUT CAKE
2½ cups cake flour
1 tablespoon baking powder
1 teaspoon salt
5 egg whites
¾ cup (1½ sticks) unsalted butter, softened
1½ cups granulated sugar
1 teaspoon vanilla extract
1 can (13.5 ounces) unsweetened coconut milk
Dark-chocolate-covered almonds, for garnish

Preheat the oven to 350°F. Grease three 8-inch round cake pans, line the bottoms with parchment paper, grease and set aside.

In a medium bowl, sift or whisk together the cake flour, baking powder and salt and set aside.

Beat the egg whites in the bowl of a stand mixer fitted with the whisk attachment until stiff peaks form. Scoop the egg whites into a bowl and set aside. Wipe the mixing bowl clean.

Beat the butter and sugar together in the bowl of a stand mixer fitted with the paddle attachment until light and fluffy, then add the vanilla.

With the mixer on low, add the flour mixture, alternating with the coconut milk until the batter is completely mixed and smooth. Use a spatula to fold in the egg whites, carefully stirring until no white streaks remain.

Divide the batter evenly among cake pans and bake for 30 minutes or until a toothpick inserted in the center of a cake comes out clean. Cool completely in the pans.

COCONUT SWISS
MERINGUE FROSTING

1 cup granulated sugar
4 egg whites
1 cup (2 sticks) unsalted butter, cubed and softened
2 cups coconut flakes, for assembly

CHOCOLATE FUDGE COATING

10 ounces high-quality semisweet chocolate,
chips or chopped
4 tablespoons (½ stick) unsalted butter
1 tablespoon light corn syrup

TIP

Short on time?
You can bake the cakes
in advance and freeze
them for later. If cooled
completely and wrapped
tightly, the unfrosted
cakes will keep in the
freezer for about
three weeks.

Freezing a cake
that's already
been frosted?
Not a good idea.

In a stand mixer bowl set over a saucepan of simmering water, whisk the sugar and egg whites until combined.

Cook over medium heat, stirring often, until the sugar is dissolved and the mixture is very warm, about 3 minutes.

Move the bowl to the stand mixer fitted with the whisk attachment, and whip on high for 5 minutes, or until cooled and stiff peaks form.

Switch from the whisk to the paddle attachment. With the mixer on medium, add in the butter, one cube at a time.

Once incorporated, continue to beat until the frosting thickens. Don't be discouraged if it looks runny. Continue to beat the frosting and after a few minutes it will magically turn from a seemingly curdled soup to a thick and silky frosting.

Combine the chocolate, butter and corn syrup into a heat-safe bowl set over a saucepan of simmering water.

Stir until chocolate is just melted, then remove from heat and continue to stir until smooth. Set aside to cool slightly.

To Assemble:
Invert the pans to release the cakes. If the tops of the cakes are rounded, use a serrated knife to level them.

Place one layer on a cake stand, then use an offset spatula to frost the top of the cake with about ⅓ cup of the Swiss Meringue. Sprinkle ½ cup of the coconut flakes on top of the frosting. Repeat with a second cake layer, frosting and another ½ cup of coconut flakes.

Top with the final cake layer. Create a thin crumb coat (pg. 33) of frosting around the cake that will seal in all the crumbs and make a smooth base for the remaining frosting. Refrigerate for about 20 minutes.

Use an offset spatula to spread on the remaining frosting. The trick to icing a cake is to remove frosting from the cake and not to add it. So start by applying a large amount of frosting on the top of the cake and spread the excess towards the edges and over the sides.

Frost the sides by holding the spatula upright with the edge against the cake. Slowly rotate the cake to create a seamless layer of frosting. Place the excess frosting back in the bowl and repeat until the entire cake is smooth.

Press the remaining 1 cup of coconut flakes around the base of the cake.

Carefully drizzle the Chocolate Fudge Coating over the top of the cake, letting it drip over the sides. Garnish with a few chocolate-covered almonds on top.

chocolate fudge

TIP

Nonpareils are perfect for coating because they're smaller than sprinkles and cover more surface area.

FUNFETTI COOKIE DOUGH CUBES

The name of this recipe contains the three most beloved words to anyone with a sweet tooth: Funfetti and cookie dough. If you aren't teeming with anticipation right now, then just shut this book and walk away. A few of you may be too ashamed to admit to loving Funfetti, claiming it's unsophisticated or meant for kids. Well I love Funfetti, and I'm not ashamed to admit it. Let your inner child come out for a while and enjoy these eggless treats. Here's a throwback to your youth that's fancy enough to serve at a dinner party. I guarantee, no one will complain about this dessert.

Makes about 36 cubes

1 cup (2 sticks) unsalted butter, softened
¾ cup granulated sugar
¾ cup light brown sugar, plus ¼ cup for coating
⅓ cup milk
1½ teaspoons vanilla extract
2½ cups all-purpose flour
¼ teaspoon baking soda
1 teaspoon salt
1 cup mini semisweet chocolate chips
½ cup rainbow sprinkles
½ cup graham cracker crumbs
½ cup rainbow nonpareils

Beat the butter, sugar and ¾ cup of the brown sugar on medium speed in the bowl of a stand mixer fitted with the paddle attachment for a few minutes, until light and fluffy.

Add milk and vanilla. With the mixer on low, add in the flour, baking soda and salt until incorporated. Stir in chocolate chips and sprinkles.

Scoop dough into an 8-inch square dish lined with plastic wrap. Smooth dough with a spatula and cover with plastic wrap. Place dough in the freezer for at least 1 hour.

Make the coating by mixing the graham cracker crumbs and the remaining ¼ cup of light brown sugar in a shallow dish. Fill another shallow dish with the rainbow nonpareils.

Remove dough from freezer and unwrap. Use a sharp knife to trim the edges and cut the dough into 1-inch cubes.

Coat all but one side in the graham cracker mixture, then coat the final side in the nonpareils.

It's unlikely they'll last that long, but these will keep in an airtight container in the refrigerator for up to a week.

PIÑATA CAKE

When I was a kid, piñatas were the unofficial requirement at every birthday celebration. My brother Dan, being the oldest and oddly overly cautious one, would make us all line up in an orderly fashion at safe distance from the piñata. (*Because, you know, accidents happen when kids are blindfolded and swinging weapons.*) Luckily, we won't need those baseball bats and broom sticks. This piñata cake doesn't need a whack; a knife's all you need to reveal the delicious candy surprise inside. Here, a spiced Mexican Chocolate Cake is covered with fondant strips that mimic the paper fringe on a piñata. As a girl who's had fiesta-themed birthday parties for as long as I can remember, this cake is a must-have. It's a double-whammy of greatness: Have your piñata and eat it, too.

YOU'LL NEED:
Mexican Chocolate cake (see recipe)
Chocolate Buttercream Frosting (see recipe)
Assorted candies (about 3 cups)
1 lb. package of colored ready-to-use fondant, at least 4 colors
Confectioners' sugar and cornstarch, for dusting

Makes one 7-by-9-inch layer cake

MEXICAN CHOCOLATE CAKE
2 cups all-purpose flour
1 cup unsweetened cocoa powder
1 teaspoon baking soda
1 teaspoon baking powder
1 teaspoon cinnamon
¼ teaspoon cayenne pepper
1 teaspoon salt
1 cup (2 sticks) unsalted butter, softened
2 cups granulated sugar
3 eggs
1 teaspoon vanilla extract
1 cup buttermilk, at room temperature
¾ cup strong coffee, at room temperature

Preheat the oven to 350°F. Grease a 13-by-18-inch sheet pan, line with parchment paper, then grease the paper.

In a large bowl, whisk or sift together the flour, cocoa powder, baking soda, baking powder, cinnamon, cayenne pepper and salt. Set aside.

In the bowl of a stand mixer fitted with the paddle attachment, cream the butter and sugar until light and fluffy. Add the eggs one at a time until fully incorporated, then mix in the vanilla.

With the mixer on low, add the flour mixture, alternating with the buttermilk until the batter is completely mixed and smooth. Slowly mix in the coffee and beat until just incorporated.

Pour into the sheet pan and bake for 25 minutes or until a toothpick inserted in the center comes out clean.

CHOCOLATE BUTTERCREAM FROSTING

3½ cups confectioners' sugar
½ cup unsweetened cocoa powder
1 cup (2 sticks) unsalted butter, softened
3 tablespoons milk
1 teaspoon vanilla extract

Sift or whisk the confectioners' sugar and cocoa powder together and set aside.

In the bowl of a stand mixer fitted with the paddle attachment, beat butter for about 30 seconds. Turn the mixer on low, then add the powdered sugar mix.

Drizzle in the milk and mix until creamy. Mix in the vanilla, then beat at medium speed for about a minute. Add more milk if needed to achieve desired consistency.

To Assemble:
Once the cake cools completely, cut the cake in half lengthwise and crosswise. You will have four pieces that are about 6½-by-8½ inches.

Place one of the rectangles on your cake stand or serving plate and frost with a thin layer of the Chocolate Buttercream Frosting. Top with a second layer of cake, frost it and top with the third cake layer.

Use a sharp knife to carefully cut the middle out of the stack, leaving a 1½-inch border of cake around the edge. Fill the cavity all the way to the top with candy!

Spread a thin layer of frosting on top of the cake, then place the remaining rectangle on top. Trim any overhanging cake so the sides are even.

Frost the entire cake with the Chocolate Buttercream Frosting and chill in the refrigerator while you prepare the fondant strips.

Lightly dust a clean work surface with a 50/50 mix of confectioners' sugar and cornstarch..

Roll the fondant to ⅛-inch thick and use a ruler and a sharp knife to cut the fondant into ½-inch-by-2-inch strips. Re-roll the scraps, cutting as many strips as you can from each color.

Take the cake out of the refrigerator. Starting from the bottom, arrange the strips in a row all around the cake. Overlap the strips slightly so none of the frosting peeks through and let strips hang off the cake slightly so they look like fringe.

Once you finish the first row, start the second row in another color. Overlap the fondant to continue the fringe look. Continue until the entire cake is covered in the strips of fondant. Use your fingers to curl up the edges of the fringe.

TIP

If you don't like the color options in the store-bought fondant, just buy white and color to your liking.

Low-fat milk works, but whole milk makes for the creamiest frosting.

CANDY BUTTONS

Of all the nostalgic candies, candy buttons reign supreme. It's incredible that something so simple could make kids (*and adults*) so happy. Bring that sublime feeling back with a little vanilla-flavored royal icing and food coloring. The color combination and pattern possibilities are endless here, but I prefer to keep things simple—just like they were in our childhood.

Keep it simple. A two-or-three-color combination can make a bold statement. Resist the urge to make the buttons in every color of the rainbow.

TIP

YOU'LL NEED:
Candy Buttons Template (pg. 158)
Lightweight white paper, cut into 2¾-by-11-inch strips
Candy Buttons (see recipe)

CANDY BUTTONS
4 cups (about 1 lb.) confectioners' sugar
3 tablespoons meringue powder
½ cup water
1 teaspoon vanilla extract
Gel food coloring

Secure the template to a work surface (the back of a sheet pan works great!) with tape, then tape the strips of white paper on top of the template.

Combine the sugar, meringue powder, water and vanilla in the bowl of a stand mixer fitted with the whisk attachment, and beat until icing is shiny and soft peaks form.

The consistency is right when you remove the whisk attachment and the peak falls onto itself. If icing is too thick, add more water, one teaspoon at a time. If it's too runny, add more confectioners' sugar.

Depending on how many colors you want, divide the icing evenly into small bowls and color with food coloring. Once colored, scoop icing into piping bags, each fitted with a size 3 tip.

Using the template as a guide, carefully pipe dots on the paper strips. Let dry completely.

Variation:
Almond or lemon extract can easily be swapped for the vanilla in this recipe.

Artistic Endeavors

Although I love to work in all artistic mediums, desserts are a clear favorite. When else can you create a beautiful piece of art—and then eat it? Paintings and sculpture look great on a pedestal or a wall, but wouldn't both be a lot more fun if they were edible? Although I occasionally paint on a traditional canvas, nowadays most of my paintbrushes are used in the kitchen instead of an art studio. Here are a few of my favorite desserts inspired by art. Whether it's a single painter, an art movement or even just the color wheel, the art world provides unlimited inspiration.

ROTHKO COOKIES

GUSTAV KLIMT TRUFFLES

POLLOCK S'MORES PIE

PAINT SWATCH PETIT FOURS

WATERCOLOR CELEBRATION CAKE

WAYNE THIEBAUD WHOOPIE PIES

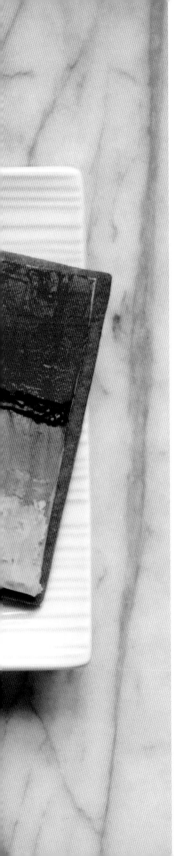

ROTHKO COOKIES

Even if you aren't artsy-fartsy, you'll probably recognize the unmistakable rectangular blocks of color in American painter Mark Rothko's work. I often see prints of his work hanging in the homes and offices of people who aren't even abstract art lovers. No matter what style of art you prefer, Rothko's work is expressive and undeniably beautiful.

For these cookies, I wanted a perfectly smooth canvas, so I covered a rich chocolate cookie with a thin layer of white fondant. Tint a simple vanilla buttercream with gel food coloring and you're only a few brushstrokes away from your own masterpiece.

Makes 18 cookies

CHOCOLATE CUTOUT COOKIES

1½ cups all-purpose flour
½ cup unsweetened cocoa powder
½ teaspoon baking soda
½ teaspoon salt
½ cup (1 stick) unsalted butter, softened
¾ cup light brown sugar
1 egg
1 teaspoon vanilla extract

Combine the flour, cocoa, baking soda and salt in a small bowl, and set aside.

In a stand mixer fitted with the paddle attachment, beat the butter and brown sugar until light and fluffy. Add the egg and vanilla and continue to mix until incorporated.

Add the flour mixture, mixing until dough just comes together. Wrap dough in plastic wrap and refrigerate for at least 2 hours, or until firm.

Preheat the oven to 350°F. Line a baking sheet with liners or parchment paper.

On a lightly floured work surface, roll out the chilled dough to about ⅛-inch thick. Use a sharp knife and a ruler to cut 3-by-4-inch rectangles. Gather and re-roll scraps to make more cookies.

Place the cookies ½ inch apart on the baking sheet. Bake for 10 minutes, then cool completely.

Lightly dust a work surface with confectioners' sugar and roll out the fondant to ⅛-inch thick. Use a sharp knife and a ruler to cut fondant rectangles that are slightly smaller than the cookies. Set aside.

Variation:
Add a teaspoon of instant espresso powder while mixing the dough for mocha-flavored cookies.

SIMPLE VANILLA BUTTERCREAM

1 cup (2 sticks) unsalted butter, softened

4 cups (about 1 lb.) confectioners' sugar

3 to 4 tablespoons milk

1 teaspoon vanilla extract

Pinch of salt

Gel food coloring

In the bowl of a stand mixer fitted with the paddle attachment, beat butter for about 30 seconds. Turn the mixer on low, then add the confectioners' sugar.

Drizzle in 3 tablespoons of the milk and mix until creamy, then add the vanilla and salt. Beat at medium speed for about a minute, adding more milk if needed to achieve desired consistency. Use food coloring to tint small batches of buttercream as desired.

To Assemble:
Use a small amount of Simple Vanilla Buttercream to stick the fondant rectangle to the cookie.

Use a clean paintbrush to paint the buttercream right onto the fondant. Now that's some tasty paint!

Keep cookies in an airtight container for up to a week.

Buttercream Variations

ALMOND
Swap the vanilla extract for 2 teaspoons of almond extract.

LEMON
Add 2 tablespoons freshly squeezed lemon juice and 1 tablespoon lemon zest.

COFFEE
Add 1 tablespoon instant espresso dissolved in 1 teaspoon boiling water.

WHITE CHOCOLATE
Add 8 ounces chopped white chocolate, melted and cooled slightly.

GUSTAV KLIMT TRUFFLES

The Austrian painter Gustav Klimt is widely known for his decorative, ornamental paintings of women. If you look closely, they almost resemble intricate pieces of jewelry, probably because Klimt often used real gold leaf in his paintings. Edible gold leaf is one of those things that, from the moment you use it, you want to put it on everything. I'm borderline obsessed with gold leaf and its "wow" factor. If it wasn't so darn expensive, I'd use it to adorn all my desserts. Klimt's most famous painting, *The Kiss*, inspired these bite-size, super luxe espresso-chocolate truffles. Topped, of course, with gold leaf. Now that's fancy.

Having trouble getting the gold leaf to stay put? Use a paintbrush to dab a small amount of water on the truffle and the gold will stick.

Makes 12 truffles

10 ounces high-quality dark chocolate, chopped or chips
½ cup heavy whipping cream
1½ teaspoons instant espresso powder
¼ cup unsweetened cocoa powder
1 sheet edible genuine gold leaf (*found at specialty baking stores or online*)

Place chocolate in a bowl and set aside. Heat the cream in a saucepan over medium heat, whisking occasionally, until very warm (but not boiling) and bubbles begin to form at the edges.

Pour the cream over the chocolate and let sit for 2 minutes.

Whisk until all the chocolate is melted and smooth, then stir in the espresso powder. If the chocolate chips aren't all melted, microwave for 20 seconds, then stir until melted.

Cover and refrigerate for about 1 hour, or until the chocolate is firm.

Line a baking sheet with parchment paper. Use a small, spring-release ice cream scoop to scoop balls of the chocolate mixture onto the baking sheet. Refrigerate for 10 minutes.

To Assemble:
Place cocoa powder in a shallow dish and set aside.

Remove the truffles from the fridge and use your hands to roll them into perfectly round balls, then roll the balls in the cocoa powder. Tap off excess cocoa powder and set onto a serving plate.

Use a small paintbrush to carefully place small pieces of gold leaf atop each truffle.

POLLOCK S'MORES PIE

I remember when I saw my first Jackson Pollock painting as a newbie art student. At the time I was a skeptic when it came to most abstract expressionist paintings and I certainly didn't think one of Pollock's signature drip paintings would change that stance. But when I approached the larger-than-life painting, *Autumn Rhythm*, displayed at the Metropolitan Museum of Art, I was blown away. At first glance I thought the dripped paint seemed a little arbitrary, almost childlike. But then I got close (*close enough to get the stink eye from a couple museum security guards*), and I began to see the layers of detail. Each brush stroke and drip had a place, and although the painting is only brown, black and white, it was incredibly complex—a true masterpiece.

I never intended to mimic Pollock's *Autumn Rhythm*, but the first time I topped a simple chocolate chess pie with all the fixins for s'mores, there was no denying the resemblance to a Pollock. It may not have a future at the Met, but it's certainly a work of art.

Makes one 9-inch pie

GRAHAM CRACKER CRUST

1½ cups graham cracker crumbs
3 tablespoons granulated sugar
5 tablespoons unsalted butter, melted
Pinch of salt

Preheat the oven to 350°F. Combine all of the ingredients in a bowl, mixing with a fork until they begin to clump together.

Firmly press the crumb mixture on the bottom and up the sides of a 9-inch pie pan and bake for 5 minutes, then set aside while you make the Chocolate Filling. Keep the oven preheated.

CHOCOLATE FILLING

1 cup granulated sugar
¼ cup unsweetened cocoa powder
2 eggs
3 tablespoons unsalted butter, melted
1 can (5 ounces) evaporated milk
1 teaspoon vanilla extract
1 teaspoon salt

In a bowl, combine all the Chocolate Filling ingredients and whisk until fully incorporated and smooth.

Pour into the graham cracker piecrust and bake at 350°F for 30 to 40 minutes, or until the filling is set around the edges and jiggles slightly in the middle. Let pie cool before topping.

TOPPING

1 heaping cup of mini marshmallows
3 graham cracker sheets, broken into 1-inch pieces
½ cup dark chocolate chips
½ cup white chocolate chips

Turn the oven on broil. Sprinkle the marshmallows and graham cracker pieces on top of the pie, then place under the broiler to toast the marshmallows. Watch carefully, this will only take a minute!

Remove from the oven and cool to room temperature. Alternatively, if you're lucky enough to own a kitchen blowtorch, use that to toast the marshmallows.

Place the dark and white chocolate in separate bowls. Heat each in the microwave for 20 seconds, then stir, repeating until the chocolate is just about melted.

Use a spoon to drizzle the chocolate all over the pie. (This is the fun part, so go ahead and get creative!) Cool to room temperature or chill before serving.

TIP Choosing colors in the same family makes tinting the fondant swatches easier.

PAINT SWATCH PETIT FOURS

Paint swatches are integral to artists, designers and interior decorators alike. They are more than just colorful strips of paper, neatly displayed at your local hardware store. Paint swatches help us dictate the mood of our environment and surroundings. The nuances in color may seem minimal, but we've all experienced a bad color choice. The walls seem to haunt us, the color growing uglier day by day. But the great thing about paint is you can always paint over it. Of course, you don't have to be a painter to appreciate a paint swatch. When I was a kid, I used to take as many swatches from the paint store as I could without getting noticed. Then at home I'd create colorful collages and garlands.

If a paint swatch was a dessert, it would without a doubt be a petit four. These tiny little cakes are coated in a vanilla glaze and each topped with a colorful swatch. They're bite-size reminders of how brilliant our color wheel really is. Plus, they offer the perfect way to match dessert with the color scheme at a baby shower or wedding. If you weren't an artist before, you certainly will be once you create these.

YOU'LL NEED:
Banana Cake (see recipe)
Petit Four Coating (see recipe)
1 lb. package of ready-to-use white rolled fondant
Gel food coloring
Confectioners' sugar and cornstarch, for dusting
Black edible ink pen (I use AmeriColor Gourmet Writers)

If blackberry jam isn't your thing, try apricot or strawberry jam instead.

Makes about 40 petit fours

BANANA CAKE

2¾ cups all-purpose flour
1 tablespoon baking powder
1 teaspoon salt
¾ cup (1½ sticks) unsalted butter, softened
2 cups granulated sugar
3 eggs
2 teaspoons vanilla extract
1½ cups buttermilk
1 cup mashed ripe bananas (about 3 bananas)
1½ cups seedless blackberry jam

Preheat the oven to 350°F. Grease a 9-by-13-inch pan, line the bottom with parchment paper, and set aside.

In a medium bowl, sift or whisk together the flour, baking powder and salt, and set aside.

Beat the butter and sugar together in the bowl of a stand mixer fitted with the paddle attachment until light and fluffy. Add the eggs, one at a time, until incorporated, then add the vanilla.

With the mixer on low, add the flour mixture, alternating with the buttermilk until the batter is completely mixed and smooth.

Stir in the mashed bananas, then pour the batter into the lined pan and bake for 40 minutes, or until a toothpick inserted in the center of the cake comes out clean.

Cool completely, then invert the cake onto a clean work surface.

Trim the edges and slice the cake horizontally into two equal layers. Spread the jam on top of one layer, then top with the other layer. Chill the cake while you make the Petit Four Coating.

PETIT FOUR COATING

6 cups confectioners' sugar
2 tablespoons light corn syrup
⅔ cup water
1 teaspoon vanilla extract

Combine all the ingredients in a saucepan and heat over medium heat until smooth and pourable.

Transfer to a bowl and set aside.

TIP Patience is a requirement when making petit fours. But once you get into a rythym coating the cakes, you'll be a pro!

MAKE THE PETIT FOURS

Place a cooling rack on top of a sheet of parchment paper and remove the cake from the fridge.

Cut the cake into 1½-by- 1½-inch squares. Carefully dip each square into the coating. Use a spoon to coat the top and any other exposed cake, then place it on the rack so the excess can drip off. If the coating begins to harden, heat it in the microwave for 15 seconds, then stir to make it pourable again.

Let the cakes set while you make the fondant paint swatch squares.

Select a few paint swatch colors and, using the food coloring, tint the fondant to match the swatches.

Lightly dust your work surface with a 50/50 mix of cornstarch and confectioners' sugar, and roll out the fondant to ⅛-inch thick. Using a ruler and a paring knife, cut 1½-by-1½-inch squares of the fondant.

Use a small amount of Petit Four Coating to attach the swatches to the petit fours.

A few years ago, I taught a cake decorating
class to two very stylish teenage girls.
Once we covered the cake in fondant, I
looked at them and excitedly announced,
"Here's your blank canvas! How would
you like to decorate it?" I had sprinkles,
assorted cookie cutters and the supplies
to make intricate sugar flowers. But these
two girls grabbed a couple paintbrushes
and declared that they wanted to
"paint" the cake. I was concerned that
the cake would look like a toddler's
finger-painting, but as I watched them
thoughtfully brush diluted food coloring
onto the cake, the result was nothing
short of stunning. Even the smallest drip
made a bold statement.

While it's important to practice restraint
when painting a cake, it's really hard
to mess up. The more diluted the food
coloring is, the more subtle the brush of
color will be. Vodka plays an important
role here, taking the place of water in
diluting the food coloring. Water would
cause the fondant to become soggy and
break down, but the vodka evaporates,
leaving only beautiful color.

WATERCOLOR CELEBRATION CAKE

YOU'LL NEED:
Vanilla Swirl Cake (see recipe)
Simple Vanilla Buttercream (see recipe)
1 lb. package of ready-to-use white rolled fondant
Confectioners' sugar and cornstarch, for dusting
Gel food coloring
Vodka

Makes one 8-inch layer cake

VANILLA SWIRL CAKE
2¾ cups all-purpose flour
1 tablespoon baking powder
1 teaspoon salt
1 cup (2 sticks) unsalted butter, softened
2 cups granulated sugar
5 eggs
2 teaspoons vanilla extract
1½ cups buttermilk
Gel food coloring

Preheat the oven to 350°F. Grease three 8-inch round cake pans, line the bottoms with parchment paper, grease and set aside.

In a medium bowl, sift or whisk together the flour, baking powder and salt, and set aside.

Beat the butter and sugar together in the bowl of a stand mixer fitted with the paddle attachment until light and fluffy. Add the eggs, one at a time, until incorporated.

Scrape down the sides of the bowl and add the vanilla. With the mixer on low, add the flour mixture, alternating with the buttermilk until the batter is completely mixed and smooth.

Divide the batter evenly among cake pans then randomly place a few drops of food coloring on top of the batter. (I used blue, teal and pink.) Use a toothpick to swirl the color into the batter.

Bake for 40 minutes or until a toothpick comes out clean. Cool completely.

SIMPLE VANILLA BUTTERCREAM
1 cup (2 sticks) unsalted butter, softened
4 cups (about 1 lb.) confectioners' sugar
3 to 4 tablespoons milk
1 teaspoon vanilla extract
Pinch of salt

In the bowl of a stand mixer fitted with the paddle attachment, beat butter for about 30 seconds. Turn the mixer on low, then add the confectioners' sugar.

Drizzle in 3 tablespoons of the milk until creamy, then add the vanilla and salt. Beat at medium speed for about a minute, adding more milk if needed to achieve desired consistency.

To Assemble:
Use a sharp serrated knife to slice each cake into two even layers. This will create six thin cake layers and will look more impressive when you cut into the cake.

Place the first layer on your cake stand and use an offset spatula to frost the top of the layer. Place the remaining half of the cake layer on top and frost the top, continuing to stack and fill all the layers.

You'll use half of the frosting to fill the cake layers and the other half to create a thin crumb coat (pg. 33) around the outside of the cake. Once the crumb coat is complete, place the cake in the refrigerator to chill while you roll out the fondant.

COVERING A CAKE IN FONDANT

Once the crumb coat has chilled, you're ready to cover the cake in fondant. Don't be intimidated at the thought of working with fondant. It's essentially just a sugar Play-Doh and, as with anything, practice makes perfect.

Lightly dust a clean workspace with a 50/50 mix of confectioners' sugar and cornstarch.

Knead the fondant to soften it up and shape into a flat disk. Use a rolling pin to roll out the fondant to ¼-inch thick, rotating the fondant as you work to keep it from sticking. Make sure to roll the fondant until it's large enough to cover the cake, sides and all.

Carefully pick up the fondant and drape it over the cake, wiping off any excess confectioners' sugar and cornstarch. Gently press the fondant so it sticks to the cake, then smooth out any bumps with your hands.

Carefully cut away any excess fondant at the bottom of the cake with a paring knife. Use a fondant smoother to finish the cake and smooth out any tricky bumps.

paint the cake

To paint the cake, place a drop of food coloring into a ramekin, then add a tablespoon of vodka; repeat with additional colors, ramekins and vodka.

Starting at the bottom, paint the food coloring on the cake with a pastry brush or a flat-edged paintbrush. If the color is too saturated, add more vodka. If the color seems too washed out, add more food coloring.

Blend the colors together to achieve a true watercolor effect. To achieve the gold finish: Use a small paintbrush to add a few drops of vodka to gold luster dust, then paint on the cake. Let the cake dry before cutting.

TIP

Less is more with watercolor. Try to apply the more saturated color at the bottom of the cake, then feather to a very light, washed out color toward the top.

If ever there was an artist who captures the beauty of a baked good, it's Wayne Thiebaud. His Pop Art cake paintings offer a slice into the sweet life of a 1960s confection. Thiebaud could be a baker himself, by the way he perfectly swirls the oil paint to mimic a luscious buttercream frosting. I find his paintings inspiring both in and out of the kitchen, but the way he uses pastel colors always leaves me craving a retro dessert. Inspired by his *Neapolitan Meringue* painting, which showcases the superstar trio of strawberry, vanilla and chocolate, I present Neapolitan whoopie pies. You can mix and match the flavors any way you like, they'll always be a delicious combo.

WHOOPIE PIES

1½ cups, plus ⅓ cups all-purpose flour
1½ teaspoons baking soda
½ teaspoon salt
½ cup (1 stick) unsalted butter, softened
¾ cup light brown sugar
1 egg
1 teaspoon vanilla extract
¾ cup buttermilk
½ cup strawberries, finely chopped
Red food coloring
¼ cup unsweetened cocoa powder
1 teaspoon strong coffee, at room temperature

VANILLA FILLING

½ cup (1 stick) unsalted butter, softened
4 ounces cream cheese, softened
4 cups (about 1 lb.) confectioners' sugar
½ teaspoon vanilla extract
Pinch of salt

Preheat oven to 375°F. Line 2 baking sheets with liners or parchment paper and set aside. Sift or whisk together 1½ cups flour, baking soda and salt in a bowl and set aside.

In the bowl of a stand mixer fitted with the paddle attachment, beat together the butter and brown sugar until light and fluffy. Add the egg, beating until combined, then add the vanilla.

Reduce speed to low and mix in flour mixture, alternating with the buttermilk, beginning and ending with the flour.

Scoop out half of the batter into a bowl and stir in the remaining ⅓ cup of flour, the strawberries and a couple drops of red food coloring. To the remaining batter in the mixer, mix in the cocoa powder and coffee.

Use a spring loaded ice cream scoop to place large tablespoons of batter about 2 inches apart onto the baking sheets. Bake for 15 to 20 minutes, or until tops spring back when touched. Set aside to cool completely while you make the Vanilla Filling.

In the bowl of a stand mixer fitted with the paddle attachment, beat butter and cream cheese for about 30 seconds.

Turn the mixer on low, then add the confectioners' sugar, vanilla and salt. Beat at medium speed for about a minute, or until smooth and creamy. Set aside.

To Assemble:
Scoop frosting into a piping bag fitted with a large star tip. Pipe filling between one chocolate and one strawberry cookie.

Store whoopie pies in an airtight container in the refrigerator for up to 3 days.

natural curiosities

Mother Nature is the best creator of all, isn't she? It only takes a few moments of observation in the great outdoors to become inspired by the unique vein patterns in leaves, the color of a newly blossomed tulip, or the microscopic detail in a snowflake. No matter the season, Mother Nature offers a pastry chef plenty of curiosities to be inspired by: edible chocolate leaves adorn the Mint Chocolate Trifle, fondant honeybees hover above the Cheesecake Bites, and the Succulent Cupcakes are so realistic looking, even you might do a double take. Mother Nature would be proud.

SUCCULENT CUPCAKES

TREE RING SPICE COOKIES

MOSS & MUSHROOM CUPCAKES

HONEYBEE CHEESECAKE BITES

MINT CHOCOLATE TRIFLE

SPICED PINECONE CAKES

SUCCULENT CUPCAKES

YOU'LL NEED:

Chocolate Cupcakes (see recipe)

Peanut Butter Buttercream Frosting (see recipe)

1 lb. package of ready-to-use white rolled fondant

Gel food coloring in electric green, black, orange and brown

Small, medium and large Petunia sugar flower cutters, ranging from 1½ to 2¾ inches wide (typically sold in a set of 5)

Purple luster dust or cocoa powder, for dusting (optional)

Confectioners' sugar and cornstarch, for dusting

Terra-Cotta Pot Template (pg. 159)

The creation of these cupcakes happened on a spring day, when I glanced over at my succulent plants perched on the window sill and thought, "Those little plants are as cute as cupcakes!" The Succulent Cupcakes they inspired are so true to life that even the fondant terra-cotta pots look authentic. The blog post I devoted to these little cacti-creations is the most popular post I've ever written; it's still getting clicks, since succulent plants remain wildly popular. I was lucky enough to remake these cupcakes on ABC's *The Chew*, leading to what I like to call my one-segment-of-daytime-television fame. *So yeah, I'm basically a mega celebrity thanks to these little plants. No photographs please. Can't you see I'm wearing my sunglasses indoors?* Make them yourself and you might be famous, too.

Makes 12 cupcakes

CHOCOLATE CUPCAKES
1¼ cups all-purpose flour
½ cup unsweetened cocoa powder
1 teaspoon baking soda
½ teaspoon salt
½ cup (1 stick) unsalted butter, softened
1 cup granulated sugar
2 eggs
1 teaspoon vanilla extract
¾ cup buttermilk
¼ cup strong coffee, at room temperature

PEANUT BUTTER BUTTERCREAM
1 cup graham cracker crumbs
4 tablespoons (½ stick) unsalted butter, softened
1 cup creamy peanut butter
2 cups confectioners' sugar
3 to 4 tablespoons milk
1 teaspoon vanilla extract

Preheat the oven to 350°F. Line a standard muffin tin with 12 cupcake liners and set aside.

In a large bowl, whisk or sift together the flour, cocoa powder, baking soda and salt. Set aside.

In the bowl of a stand mixer fitted with the paddle attachment, cream the butter and sugar until light and fluffy. Add the eggs one at a time, until fully incorporated, then add the vanilla.

With the mixer on low, add the flour mixture, alternating with the buttermilk until the batter is completely mixed and smooth. Slowly add in the coffee and beat until incorporated.

Divide the batter into the muffin tin, filling each cup about ¾ full. If you have a small amount of extra batter, don't overfill the cups, just make more cupcakes!

Bake for 15 to 20 minutes or until a toothpick inserted in the center of a cupcake comes out clean. Set aside to cool.

Place graham cracker crumbs in a shallow dish and set aside.

In the bowl of a stand mixer fitted with the paddle attachment, beat the butter and peanut butter for about 30 seconds. Turn the mixer on low, then add the confectioners' sugar.

Drizzle in 3 tablespoons of the milk until creamy, then add the vanilla. Beat at medium speed for about a minute, adding more milk if needed to achieve desired consistency.

Use a small offset spatula to spread icing onto the cupcakes, and then coat with graham cracker crumbs. Set cupcakes aside.

TO MAKE THE SUCCULENTS:

Prepare a clean, non-stick workspace to cut and color fondant.

Divide the white fondant in half. Tint one half green by kneading several drops of electric green gel food coloring and a tiny drop of black into the fondant. Continue to knead, adding more coloring if needed to achieve the perfect shade of succulent leaf green. It helps to have a real succulent plant nearby for reference.

Tint the remaining half of fondant with several drops of orange and a few drops of brown. Add more coloring if needed to achieve the perfect terra-cotta color. Wrap this half of the fondant tightly with plastic wrap and set aside for later. The color will become more vibrant as the fondant sits.

Lightly dust your work surface with a 50/50 mix of cornstarch and confectioners' sugar and roll the green fondant out to ⅛-inch thick. Use the petunia cutters to cut as many leaves as you can in assorted sizes. For 12 cupcakes, you'll need at least 12 large, 12 medium and 24 small leaves.

Press the large leaves into the mini muffin tin to harden slightly. Place the medium leaves cupped inside the larger ones. Collect the scraps and pinch a pea-sized amount of fondant off, rolling into a ball. Repeat until you have at least 12 small balls.

Build your succulents from the inside out. Begin by wrapping a small petunia leaf around a pea-sized ball of fondant. Use the tiniest dab of water so the fondant will stick. The leaves should overlap, covering the ball to mimic the look of budding leaves.

Loosely wrap the "bud" in another small petunia leaf and set inside of one of the medium leaves in the muffin tin. Your leaves should now resemble a succulent plant.

Once the leaf cutouts are stiff enough to hold a cup shape, use a small amount of frosting to ensure all the cupped leaves stick together. Use a paintbrush to dust the edges of the succulent with purple luster dust or cocoa powder, then set aside. Succulents can be made in advance, just store them in an airtight container in a dry place.

TO MAKE THE TERRA-COTTA POT:

Clip out the terra-cotta pot template (pg. 159). Lightly dust your work surface with a 50/50 mix of cornstarch and confectioners' sugar and roll the fondant out to ⅛-inch thick. Use a sharp knife to cut out 12 fondant pots for each cupcake.

Remove the liners from the cupcakes and spread a thin layer of buttercream around the cupcake, then wrap with the fondant. The lip of the pot can be achieved by wrapping a ¼-inch wide strip of fondant around the top of the cupcake. Use a small amount of frosting to make sure it sticks.

To finish, place the succulent on top of the cupcake with a small amount of buttercream.

TREE RING SPICE COOKIES

Young couples used to say I love you by carving their initials in a tree, which seems infinitely more romantic than changing your online status to "In a relationship." I made these cookies for my husband, carved our initials in the dough and baked my way right into his heart. He skeptically took a bite of the cookie, insisting it looked too much like a real wood cross-section to taste good. To his surprise (*and delight*) the cookie wasn't tree bark at all. It was the most fragrant and delicious combination of cardamom and gingerbread flavors. Maybe now if you fall in love, you'll set your status to "In the kitchen," then say I love you with a trunk cookie.

Makes 2 dozen cookies

YOU'LL NEED:
Cardamom-Honey Cookie Dough for the light rings (see recipe)
Gingerbread Cookie Dough for the dark rings (see recipe)
1 egg, lightly beaten
1 cup sliced almonds, roughly chopped
2 tablespoons turbinado sugar
Brown edible ink pen (I use AmeriColor Gourmet Writers)

CARDAMOM-HONEY COOKIE DOUGH

2 cups all-purpose flour, plus more for dusting

½ teaspoon ground cardamom

¼ teaspoon salt

½ teaspoon baking soda

½ cup (1 stick) unsalted butter, softened

⅓ cup granulated sugar

¼ cup honey

1 egg

1 teaspoon vanilla extract

In a bowl, whisk or sift together the flour, cardamom, salt and baking soda, then set aside.

In the bowl of a stand mixer fitted with the paddle attachment, beat the butter and sugar on medium speed until light and fluffy. Add the honey, egg and vanilla. Continue mixing on medium speed until well blended.

Slowly add the flour mixture on low speed until the dough just comes together. Scoop out the dough onto a sheet of plastic wrap and smooth into a flattened disk. Wrap tightly and refrigerate until chilled, at least 2 hours.

TIP

Plan ahead. Dough can be refrigerated for up to 3 days or frozen for 1 month.

GINGERBREAD COOKIE DOUGH

2 cups all-purpose flour, plus more for dusting

½ teaspoon salt

½ teaspoon baking soda

½ teaspoon ground cinnamon

½ teaspoon ground ginger

½ teaspoon ground nutmeg

½ cup (1 stick) unsalted butter, softened

½ cup light brown sugar

¼ cup light molasses

1 egg, beaten

1 teaspoon vanilla extract

In a bowl, whisk or sift together the flour, salt, baking soda, cinnamon, ginger and nutmeg. Set aside.

In the bowl of a stand mixer fitted with the paddle attachment, beat the butter and brown sugar on medium speed until light and fluffy. Add the molasses, egg and vanilla, and continue to beat until well blended.

Add the flour mixture and mix on low speed until the dough just comes together. Scoop out the dough ball onto a sheet of plastic wrap and smooth into a flattened disk. Wrap tightly and refrigerate until chilled, at least 2 hours.

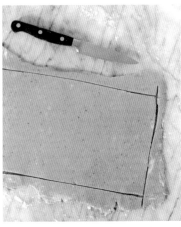

To Assemble:

Remove the chilled dough discs from the fridge. Roll out half of the chilled cardamom dough on a liberally floured work surface to ⅛-inch thick. Use a ruler and a sharp knife to cut a 12-by-6-inch rectangle, then carefully set it aside on a large sheet of parchment paper. Gather scraps and set aside.

Next, roll out half of the gingerbread dough and cut just like you did with the cardamom dough. Place this rectangle directly on top of the other one.

Repeat the process until you have six alternating layers, or no scraps remain. It's OK if the rectangles aren't perfect or the dough tears a bit—it's supposed to look natural!

Once all the dough is stacked, start with a long side and tightly roll the rectangle into a log. (Use the parchment paper to help get the roll started.) Wrap the dough in the parchment paper and chill in the freezer until firm, about 30 minutes.

Preheat the oven to 350°F. Line a baking sheet with a liner or parchment paper. Remove the dough from freezer and unwrap.

Use a pastry brush to cover the log with the beaten egg, then roll in the almonds and sprinkle with turbinado sugar so the entire log is covered. Slice the log into ¼-inch thick rounds, then transfer the rounds to the baking sheet. Use a sharp knife to carve initials into the top of the cookies.

Bake for 12 minutes or until edges are golden. Cool cookies completely, then use the brown edible ink pen to darken the carvings.

The first time I made meringue mushrooms, I was so excited that I giddily made several more batches. They look so real, and I've never met someone who wasn't impressed by them. A little piped meringue and a dusting of cocoa powder bring these 'shrooms to life atop a Pistachio Cupcake. The pistachio cake adds just the right amount of earthy flavor and doubles as the Moss Crumb topping. White Chocolate Buttercream ties it all together, making these cupcakes a true showstopper, certainly a work of art.

MOSS & MUSHROOM CUPCAKES

Makes 13 cupcakes

PISTACHIO CUPCAKES

1½ cups all-purpose flour
1½ teaspoons baking powder
1½ cups shelled salted pistachios
½ cup (1 stick) unsalted butter, softened
1 cup granulated sugar
2 eggs
1 teaspoon vanilla extract
⅔ cup milk
Green gel food coloring

Note: If your pistachios are unsalted, add ½ teaspoon of salt to the batter.

WHITE CHOCOLATE BUTTERCREAM

8 ounces white chocolate (the real stuff, not white candy melts), chips or chopped
½ cup (1 stick) unsalted butter, softened
1 cup confectioners' sugar
1 teaspoon vanilla extract
Pinch of salt

YOU'LL NEED:
Pistachio Cupcakes (see recipe)
White Chocolate Buttercream (see recipe)
Moss Crumb Topping (see: To Assemble)
Meringue Mushrooms (see pg. 99)

Preheat the oven to 350°F and line 16 cups in two standard muffin tins.

Whisk together the flour and baking powder in a bowl and set aside. Use a mini food processor to grind 1 cup of the pistachios until very fine, then add to the flour mixture. Coarsely chop the remaining ½ cup of pistachios and set aside for assembly.

In the bowl of a stand mixer fitted with the paddle attachment, beat the butter and sugar until light and fluffy. Add the eggs, one at a time, beating until just incorporated, then add the vanilla.

Add the flour mixture, alternating with the milk until the batter is completely incorporated. Add a couple drops of green food coloring and beat until the color is even.

Divide the batter into the muffin tin, filling each cup about ¾ full. Bake for 15 minutes or until a toothpick inserted in the center of a cupcake comes out clean.

Microwave the white chocolate in a heat-safe bowl for 20 seconds, then stir; repeat until the chocolate is just about melted. Set aside to cool slightly.

In the bowl of a stand mixer fitted with the paddle attachment, beat the butter until creamy. Beat in the melted white chocolate.

Turn the mixer to low, and add the confectioners' sugar, vanilla and salt. Mix until light and fluffy.

To Assemble:
To make the Moss Crumb Topping remove the liners from three cooled cupcakes and crumble the cake into a shallow bowl. Set aside.

Use an offset spatula to frost the cupcakes with White Chocolate Buttercream. Top with the Moss Crumb Topping, a few chopped pistachios and the Meringue Mushrooms.

HONEYBEE CHEESECAKE BITES

Honeybees must be bakers at heart, because honey adds the most delicate sweetness to desserts, nearly eliminating the need for sugar. These Honeybee Cheesecake Bites are no exception, utilizing the delicious honey those bees worked so hard to produce. While honey makes them uniquely sweet, the Spun Sugar Nest and Fondant Honeybees make them the fanciest dessert on the block. Almonds give the graham cracker crust a nuttiness that pairs seamlessly with the honey cheesecake. These might just be too cute to eat, but you'll devour them anyway.

Make the cheesecakes the day before and refrigerate them in an airtight container.

Use the bottom of a ½-cup measuring cup to press the crumbs into the muffin tin.

Makes 12 mini cheesecakes

HONEY CHEESECAKE BITES

1 cup graham cracker crumbs
¼ cup sliced almonds, finely chopped
3 tablespoons granulated sugar
5 tablespoons unsalted butter, melted
Pinch of salt
16 ounces (2 packages) cream cheese, room temperature
⅓ cup honey
2 eggs
1 teaspoon lemon zest
1 teaspoon vanilla extract

Preheat the oven to 350°F and heavily grease a 12-cup muffin tin or line with cupcake liners. In a bowl, combine the graham cracker crumbs, chopped almonds, sugar, butter and salt, mixing until they clump together. Evenly press the crumb mixture into the bottoms and about half way up the sides of the muffin cups.

Bake for 10 minutes, or until crusts turn golden brown. Cool to room temperature while you make the filling.

In the bowl of a stand mixer fitted with the paddle attachment, beat the cream cheese and honey at medium speed until smooth. Add in the eggs, lemon zest and vanilla, and beat until fully incorporated and creamy.

Divide the cheesecake batter into the cups, bake for 15 minutes, then set aside to cool. Once at room temperature, cover and refrigerate while you make the Sugar Nests (pg. 98) and Fondant Honeybees.

FONDANT HONEYBEES

1 small package of yellow fondant
1 small package of black fondant
Sliced almonds
Black edible ink pen (I use AmeriColor Gourmet Writers)

Roll a dime-size amount of yellow fondant into an egg shape. Roll very thin strands of black fondant to create two rings around the yellow egg.

Stick a sliced almond into either side to create wings, then use the black edible ink marker to add eyes.

Fondant Honeybees can be made in advance and kept in a dry place.

SPUN SUGAR NESTS

2 cups granulated sugar
3 tablespoons light corn syrup
½ cup water

In a saucepan over medium heat, bring the sugar, corn syrup and water to a simmer. When all of the sugar has dissolved, increase the heat to high and boil for about 7 minutes, or until the sugar just begins to turn a golden color. Remove from the heat and carefully tilt the saucepan to swirl caramelized sugar to mix. Set aside and wait a few minutes for all the bubbles to subside. The sugar is ready to "spin" when a fork dipped in creates long strands.

Cover your work surface with plenty of parchment paper. (Things can get messy with sugar flying all over the place!) Then set a large bowl on your workspace.

To make the nest, dip the tines of a fork into the sugar and wave it back and forth over the bowl. The sugar will create long, thin strands that drape over the bowl. When enough strands have accumulated, carefully lift them off the bowl and form into a round nest, then set aside. It's important to work quickly, so the sugar doesn't harden before you form it into nests.

Repeat with the remaining sugar until you have enough nests for all the cheesecake bites. If the sugar begins to harden, just place it over low heat until it's pliable enough to work with again. Keep the nests in a dry place; any moisture can cause them to melt.

To Assemble:

Remove the cheesecakes from the muffin tin. Place one Spun Sugar Nest on top of a Honey Cheesecake Bite, then arrange Fondant Bees in each sugar nest.

MERINGUE MUSHROOMS

3 egg whites
¾ cup granulated sugar
Pinch of salt
2 ounces semisweet chocolate
Cocoa powder, for dusting

Preheat oven to 200°F. Line a baking sheet with a liner or parchment paper and set aside.

Place egg whites in the bowl of a stand mixer fitted with the whisk attachment. Beat on high speed until white and foamy.

Slowly pour the sugar into the bowl, mixing on high speed, until stiff peaks form. Add in the salt.

Transfer the meringue to a piping bag fitted with a ½-inch round tip. To pipe the mushroom caps, squeeze out 1½-inch wide mounds of meringue onto the prepared baking sheet. Pull bag off to the side to avoid making peaks on the top. If peaks remain, dip your fingertip in water and lightly tap them down.

For the stems, pipe out a small amount of meringue onto the baking sheet and pull the bag straight up. They should resemble candy kisses about 1 inch high. You'll want to pipe equal amounts of caps and stems.

Use a sifter to lightly dust the cocoa powder over the stems and caps. Bake the meringue mushrooms for about 1 hour and 30 minutes, or until dry.

Assemble the Meringue Mushrooms:
Microwave the chocolate in a heat-safe bowl for 20 seconds, then stir; repeating until the chocolate is just about melted.

Use a small offset spatula to spread chocolate on the flat under-side of the mushroom cap. Cut off the pointed ends of the stems, then attach stems to caps using the melted chocolate.

Set the assembled mushrooms aside until the chocolate hardens. Store mushrooms in an airtight container in a cool, dry place for up to a week.

TIP
Make some mushrooms smaller than others to make them look more authentic. Then top each cupcake with two mushrooms of varied sizes.

When it comes to no-fuss desserts that really impress, nothing beats a trifle. Basically, it's a delicious tower of Mint Whipped Cream, Chocolate Crumble and a Mint Chocolate Pudding. Top it with a bouquet of Chocolate Mint Leaves and you've got yourself one gorgeous dessert. If you ask me, the real star of this trifle is the mint chocolate leaves, which inspired the entire recipe. I hate to pick favorites, but this trifle might seriously be the best dessert ever.

TIP

Make the crumble, pudding and mint leaves in advance. When it's time to assemble the trifle, just whip up the cream and your trifle will come together in no time.

MINT CHOCOLATE TRIFLE

MINT CHOCOLATE PUDDING

4 egg yolks
½ cup granulated sugar
1 pint (16 ounces) heavy whipping cream
4 ounces high-quality dark chocolate,
chopped or chips
½ teaspoon peppermint extract
Pinch of salt

MINT WHIPPED CREAM

1 pint (16 ounces) cold heavy whipping cream
¼ cup confectioners' sugar
¼ teaspoon peppermint extract
Green gel food coloring

CHOCOLATE MINT LEAVES

2 dozen fresh mint leaves, the larger the better
½ cup dark chocolate chips
Small paintbrush

YOU'LL NEED:
Mint Chocolate Pudding (see recipe)
Chocolate Crumble (pg. 44)
Chocolate Mint Leaves (see recipe)
Mint Whipped Cream (see recipe)

Makes 8 servings

In a large mixing bowl, whisk together egg yolks and sugar.

Heat the cream in a saucepan over medium heat, whisking occasionally, until very warm (but not boiling) and bubbles begin to form at the edges. Remove from heat, add the chocolate and whisk until all the chocolate is melted and incorporated.

Slowly pour the chocolate mixture into the egg mixture, whisking constantly. (Make sure you pour slowly! You don't want to scramble those yolks.) Return mix to saucepan and set over medium-low heat.

Whisk constantly for about five minutes, or until mixture is thick enough to coat the back of a spoon.

Stir in the peppermint extract and salt, then pour pudding into a bowl and cover with plastic wrap. The plastic wrap should touch the pudding surface to prevent skin from forming. Refrigerate overnight, or until completely chilled.

Beat the cream and sugar in the bowl of a stand mixer fitted with the whisk attachment. Start on medium so the cream doesn't splatter everywhere, then turn it to high once the mixture starts to thicken.

Add the peppermint extract and several drops of green food coloring, then beat until stiff peaks form.

Cover with plastic wrap and keep chilled until it's time to assemble the trifle.

Microwave the chocolate in a heat-safe bowl for 20 seconds, then stir; repeat until the chocolate is just about melted.

Use the paintbrush to paint the chocolate on the underside of the leaf, making sure to get a thick coating. Let chocolate harden in a cool, dry place.

When the chocolate is fully hardened, carefully peel the stem of the leaf away from the chocolate. Leaves can be made days in advance, just store in an airtight container in a cool, dry place.

To Assemble:
Starting with one-third of the pudding, create an even layer at the bottom of a small trifle dish.

Next, spread one-third of the chocolate crumble, then top with whipped cream. Repeat, starting with the pudding again, until the dish is almost full. When you reach the top of the dish, finish with the chocolate mint leaves. Serve chilled.

spice cakes are adorned with sliced almonds and instantly transformed into realistic-looking pinecones. While they're perfect as individual desserts at any holiday or winter party, they could easily top a rustic cake at an outdoor wedding. No matter how you serve them, they're delicious, but nothing pairs better with this spice cake than a cup of strong coffee.

SPICED PINECONE CAKES

Makes 6 individual cakes

SPICED PINECONE CAKES

1½ cups all-purpose flour

1½ teaspoons baking powder

½ teaspoon salt

½ teaspoon cinnamon

¼ teaspoon ginger

¼ teaspoon cardamom

¼ teaspoon nutmeg

½ cup (1 stick) unsalted butter, softened

1 cup granulated sugar

2 eggs

1 teaspoon vanilla extract

⅔ cup buttermilk

3 ounces cream cheese, softened

1 cup confectioners' sugar, plus more for dusting

1 tablespoon milk

2 (6 ounce) bags of sliced almonds

Candied rosemary (see recipe)

CANDIED ROSEMARY

1¼ cups superfine granulated sugar

½ cup water

3–6 sprigs of rosemary

Don't toss that rosemary simple syrup! Use it to make a delicious herbaceous cocktail, like a rosemary gin and tonic. — TIP

Preheat the oven to 350°F. Grease a 9-by-13-inch pan, line the bottom with parchment paper and set aside.

In a medium bowl, sift or whisk together the flour, baking powder, salt, cinnamon, ginger, cardamom and nutmeg, and set aside.

In the bowl of a stand mixer fitted with the paddle attachment, beat the butter and sugar until light and fluffy. Add the eggs, one at a time, beating until just incorporated. Then add the vanilla.

With the mixer on low, add the flour mixture, alternating with the buttermilk until the batter is completely mixed and smooth.

Pour the batter into the pan and bake for 20 minutes, or until a toothpick inserted in the center of the cake comes out clean. Cool completely, then crumble the cake into a large bowl and set aside.

Line a baking sheet with wax or parchment paper and set aside. Combine the cream cheese, 1 cup confectioners' sugar and the milk in a large bowl, and mix until smooth and creamy.

Add the cream cheese mixture to the crumbled cake and stir until fully incorporated. (You may want to use clean hands here, as it's much easier.) The cake crumbs should clump together and hold its shape.

Scoop out a handful of the crumb mixture and mold it into a large egg shape. Place the cake standing up on the lined baking sheet and repeat with the remaining crumb mixture. You should have six cakes. Chill for about 10 minutes to firm.

Bring 1 cup of the sugar and the water to a boil in a saucepan. Place the remaining sugar in a shallow dish and set aside. Add the rosemary sprigs and boil until the liquid reduces to a syrup, or about 3 minutes.

Use tongs to remove the rosemary sprigs from the saucepan, tapping off any excess liquid, then dredge through the remaining sugar.

Set aside on a sheet of parchment paper for about an hour to dry.

To Assemble:
Starting at the bottom, stick the almonds (pointy side in) into a cake to create a row around the entire cake.

Continue to create rows, overlapping the almonds, until the whole cake is covered and resembles a pinecone. Serve with a sprig of candied rosemary and a light dusting of confectioners' sugar.

Sweet & Boozy

This chapter is just as it sounds: Each and every dessert features alcohol. Why? you ask. Well why not? Booze comes in so many delicious variations; it just makes sense to pair them with dessert. If your favorite cocktail was a dessert, what would it be? I like to think an old fashioned would be an orange-scented cherry pie spiked with bourbon. A piña colada would take form in an iconic pineapple upside down coconut cake that gets its kick from dark rum. And here's an unexpected perk of turning cocktails into confections: In addition to crafting mouth-watering desserts, you'll also bake your way to a fully stocked liquor cabinet, as these recipes only call for small amounts of alcohol. Get out your ID—you'll need it to get through this chapter.

MOJITO GRANITA

IRISH CREAM MARSHMALLOWS

"OLD FASHIONED" MINI PIES

BUBBLY POP SHOTS

PIÑA COLADA UPSIDE DOWN CAKE

LIMONCELLO TART

RED WINE PLUM COBBLER

MOJITO GRANITA

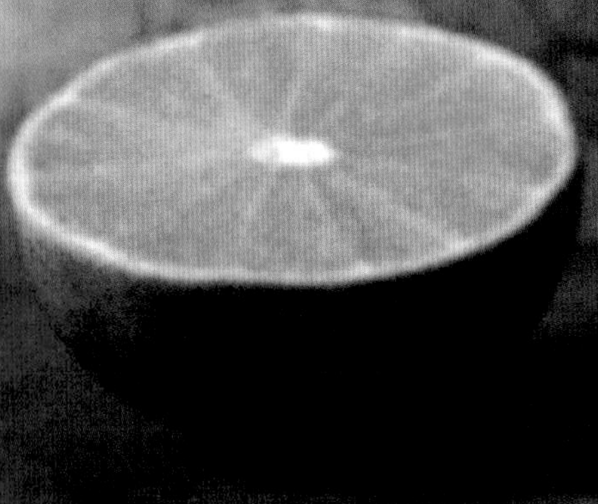

In the world of cocktails, the mojito is that friend you love to hang out with—always a good time, lighthearted, loves to dance and knows where the party's at. Maybe it's the tartness of the limes or the herbal notes from the mint, but I couldn't possibly love this drink any more. I adore the mojito so much I've turned it into a dessert. The truth is you could probably turn any cocktail into a granita. But the mojito is especially delicious frozen and it's so perfectly refreshing. This friend's a keeper.

Makes 8 servings

¾ cup granulated sugar
1 tablespoon lime zest
½ cup fresh lime juice
3 cups water
½ cup white rum
1 cup rinsed mint leaves (reserve the best leaves for garnish)

Combine the sugar, lime zest and lime juice in a small bowl. Stir until sugar is dissolved, then pour into a blender.

Add the water, rum and mint leaves to the blender, and puree for about 20 seconds or until the mint is chopped into little bits.

Pour the liquid into a metal or glass baking dish, cover with plastic wrap and place in the freezer. After about 1½ hours, use a fork to scrape and break up all the frozen parts. Cover and return to the freezer.

Wait another hour and repeat the scraping so the ice breaks into flakes. After one more hour, scrape your granita once more with the fork, then it's ready to serve.

Serve in small bowls or cocktail glasses with the reserved mint leaves. Keep leftovers covered in the freezer for about a week.

IRISH CREAM MARSHMALLOWS

If you're a fan of an Irish coffee, you'll love these marshmallows. In fact, you'll wonder why you haven't been spiking your marshmallows all along. Irish cream is smooth and pairs perfectly with a sweet marshmallow. And there are limitless variations with marshmallows, so once you master the basic recipe, you can get really creative with flavors. Toss a few in a cup of hot chocolate and these fluffy treats will melt away any winter blues.

Makes about 30 marshmallows

3 envelopes of unflavored gelatin
½ cup Baileys Irish Cream
2 cups granulated sugar
¾ cups light corn syrup
¼ teaspoon salt
¼ cup water
1 teaspoon vanilla extract
Confectioners' sugar, for dusting and dredging

In the bowl of a stand mixer fitted with the whisk attachment, sprinkle the gelatin over the Baileys and let sit for 5 minutes.

In a medium saucepan, heat the sugar, corn syrup, salt and water over medium heat, and stir constantly until it comes to a boil. Allow mixture to boil for about one minute, then turn off heat.

Carefully pour the hot syrup into the Baileys mixture and mix on high. Add the vanilla and beat for 12 to 15 minutes, or until mixture has thickened and cooled.

Line a 9-inch-square dish with greased plastic wrap and liberally dust with confectioners' sugar. Evenly pour the marshmallow mixture into the pan, dust with more confectioners' sugar, and cover with plastic wrap. Let marshmallows sit overnight.

Uncover and flip marshmallow block onto a work surface dusted with confectioners' sugar. Using a clean pair of kitchen scissors, cut into equal 1 ½-inch cubes. Coat remaining sides of marshmallows in confectioners' sugar and tap to remove excess. Store in an airtight container for up to a week.

"OLD FASHIONED" MINI PIES

The old fashioned is arguably one of the most timeless and beloved cocktails. In fact, it's seen quite the resurgence in popularity over the past few years. Whether the old fashioned will become as popular as pie remains to be seen, but there's no denying that this cocktail would taste lovely in pie form. These mini pies are a twist on a classic cherry pie, spiked with bourbon and a hint of orange. The old fashioned is truly America's cocktail, and it goes without saying that cherry pie is America's dessert. These two are clearly meant for each other.

Makes 12 mini pies

WALNUT PIE CRUST

1 cup walnuts
2½ cups all-purpose flour
1 tablespoon granulated sugar
1 teaspoon salt
1 cup (2 sticks) cold unsalted butter, cut into ½-inch cubes
⅓ cup ice water

CHERRY-BOURBON FILLING

5 cups fresh or frozen dark cherries, pitted
1 cup granulated sugar
4 tablespoons fresh orange juice
2 teaspoons orange zest
2 tablespoons cornstarch
⅓ cup bourbon

1 egg, beaten
Turbinado sugar

TIP

Make sure your butter is very cold. Those visible chunks release steam as the pie bakes, and steam creates flaky layers in your crust.

Use a smaller circle cutter to trim the excess lattice dough off each pie.

Use a food processor or knife to finely chop the walnuts, then toss in a large bowl.

Add the flour, sugar, salt and butter. Use a pastry blender or large fork to cut the butter cubes into the dry ingredients, working quickly and incorporating all of the flour mixture until the butter pieces are the size of peas.

Slowly drizzle the ice water into the flour mixture and mix until the dough pulls together. Divide into two disks and wrap each one tightly in plastic wrap. Shaping your pie dough into even, flat disks before you chill them will make rolling them out much easier.

Chill in the fridge for at least two hours, or overnight.

In a saucepan set over medium heat, combine the cherries, sugar, orange juice and zest. Sprinkle in the cornstarch, stir to combine and simmer for about 10 minutes, or until filling thickens.

Turn off the heat and stir in the bourbon. Set aside to cool.

To Assemble:
Preheat the oven to 400°F and heavily grease a 12-cup muffin tin.

Remove the disks of pie dough from the fridge and unwrap. On a floured work surface, roll dough to ⅛-inch thickness. Use an inverted glass or a round cutter to cut 4-inch circles.

Press and form dough circles into the greased muffin tins. Generously spoon filling into the cups, making sure to fill the cups with plenty of cherries. Place muffin tin in the refrigerator while you make the lattice tops.

Gather any scraps, add them to the remaining dough, re-roll and cut ¼-inch strips to create the lattice tops. Lay three strips on top of the cup in one direction, then weave in three strips perpendicular to the first three.

Press the edges of the lattice tops into the dough cups and remove any excess dough. Brush with the beaten egg and sprinkle with turbinado sugar.

Bake the pies for 20 minutes, or until the crust is golden brown. Once cooled, use a butter knife to gently pop the pies out of the muffin cups. Serve warm or at room temperature.

BUBBLY
POP SHOTS

Don't wait for New Year's Eve or the Fourth of July to make these festive Jell-O shots. There's always a reason to celebrate and the time to pop that bottle of bubbly is now. This festive dessert takes the seemingly low brow (*Ahem, sorry Jell-O shots.*) and classes it up with prosecco. The Pop Rocks add a celebratory spark and bring you right back to the days when downing an entire pouch of Pop Rocks made you a bad ass. These little poppers are a guaranteed crowd-pleaser.

Makes about 2 dozen

3 envelopes unflavored gelatin
2 cups sparkling wine, preferably prosecco
3 tablespoons granulated sugar
3 packets of Pop Rocks candy, or other "exploding" candy

In a small saucepan, sprinkle the gelatin over 1 cup of the prosecco and let stand for 2 minutes.

Turn heat on low, add the sugar, and stir until dissolved. Remove from heat and stir in the remaining prosecco. Cool to room temperature.

Transfer gelatin mixture into a loaf pan lined with plastic wrap and refrigerate for 3 hours, or until the gelatin sets.

Carefully lift the plastic wrap out of the pan, place the gelatin on a flat surface, and cut into triangles or cubes. Just before serving, sprinkle with Pop Rocks.

PIÑA COLADA UPSIDE DOWN CAKE

Put your blender and umbrella straws away, this piña colada cake is best enjoyed with a fork. This dessert celebrates the vintage pineapple upside down cake and welcomes a little Caribbean flair with the addition of rum and coconut. One bite and you'll be swept away to a serene beach, toes in the sand and hair blowing in the wind. Or at least you'll feel that way.

TIP
Toast the coconut in advance in the toaster oven.

Makes 1 loaf

1 cup coconut flakes
1½ cups all-purpose flour
1½ teaspoons baking powder
½ teaspoon salt
1½ sticks unsalted butter, softened
1 cup light brown sugar
1 small can of pineapple rings
2 eggs
¾ cup unsweetened coconut milk
¼ cup dark rum

Preheat the oven to 350°F. Evenly spread the coconut out on a baking sheet and bake in the oven for 6 to 8 minutes, or until it's nice and toasty. Set aside to cool and keep the oven preheated at 350°F.

Combine flour, baking powder and salt in a bowl, and set aside.

Melt ½ stick of butter in the microwave and pour into a large greased loaf pan. Sprinkle ½ cup brown sugar on top of the butter, then arrange the pineapple slices into the pan. You can overlap the rings, or break them in half and create a pattern. Set aside.

In the bowl of a stand mixer fitted with the paddle attachment, cream the remaining stick of butter and the remaining ½ cup brown sugar until light and fluffy. Add the eggs, one at a time.

With the mixer on low, add the flour mixture, alternating with the coconut milk. Add the rum, ½ cup of the toasted coconut flakes and beat until batter is fully incorporated, about 10 seconds.

Pour batter into the loaf pan and bake for 45 minutes, or until a toothpick inserted in the center of the cake comes out clean. If the edges begin to brown too much towards the end of baking, cover the cake with foil.

Cool to room temperature, then run a knife around the sides of the pan and flip onto a serving plate. Sprinkle with remaining toasted coconut flakes and enjoy!

LIMONCELLO TART

When my husband and I visited the Amalfi Coast on our honeymoon, we were pleasantly surprised to discover the love affair Italians have with their local lemons. It just so happens that lemons are my absolute favorite, so I too, found myself enamored with the larger-than-life lemons native to the Amalfi Coast. It was there that I also tried my first sip of the deliciously tart liqueur limoncello. When life gives you lemons, you make limoncello. When life gives you limoncello, you make something better—this lemon tart.

LEMON TART CRUST

1¼ cups all-purpose flour

2 teaspoons granulated sugar

¼ teaspoon salt

1 teaspoon lemon zest

½ cup (1 stick) cold unsalted butter, cut into ½-inch cubes

2½ tablespoons ice water

In a large bowl, combine the flour, sugar, salt and lemon zest.

Use a pastry blender or large fork to cut the butter cubes into the flour, working quickly and incorporating all of the flour mixture until the butter pieces are the size of tiny peas.

Slowly drizzle the ice water into the flour mixture, mixing until the dough pulls together. Evenly press dough into the bottom and up the sides of a greased 9-inch tart pan and freeze for 15 minutes.

Preheat the oven to 350°F. Remove the chilled tart pan from the freezer and prick the dough with a fork several times.

Set the tart pan on a baking sheet and bake for 15 minutes. Let the tart shell cool. Keep the oven preheated at 350°F.

TART FILLING

2 egg yolks

2 eggs

1 cup granulated sugar

½ cup fresh lemon juice

⅓ cup limoncello

½ cup (1 stick) unsalted butter, cubed

In a saucepan set over medium-low heat, combine the egg yolks, eggs and sugar, and whisk until incorporated.

Add in the lemon juice and limoncello, stirring constantly until thickened, about 8 minutes. Strain into a clean bowl and stir in the cubes of butter until completely melted.

Pour filling into tart shell and bake for 20 minutes, or until filling sets around the edges.

CANDIED LEMONS

2 large lemons, rinsed

2 cups granulated sugar

1 cup water

Using a sharp knife, slice the lemons into very thin slices and remove any seeds.

Bring the sugar and water to a boil in a saucepan. Once all the sugar has dissolved, reduce the heat to low, add lemon slices and simmer for 30 minutes.

Use tongs to carefully remove the lemons and place on a baking sheet lined with parchment paper to cool. Leftover candied lemons can be refrigerated in an airtight container for up to a month.

To Assemble:

Top tart with Candied Lemons and serve chilled or at room temperature.

Keep tart covered in the refrigerator for up to 3 days.

TIP — Don't toss the candied lemon syrup! Make lemon drop cocktails, or drizzle it on a basic yellow cake for a citrus twist.

RED WINE PLUM COBBLER

Red wine meets its match in this delicious plum cobbler. The wine pairs perfectly with the plums (*Obviously!*) and the tartness is offset by the crumbly butter topping. It's best to use a cast iron skillet, which doubles as an adorably rustic serving dish, for this easy one-pan dessert. The best part about this recipe is that it only needs one cup of wine, so you can drink the rest while you cook.

No cast iron skillet? Cook the filling in a saucepan instead, then transfer to a baking dish.

Makes one 10-inch cobbler

PLUM FILLING
5 ripe plums, pitted and sliced into wedges
1 cup light brown sugar
1 cup dry red wine (I like to use a Beaujolais or Cabernet Sauvignon)
1 tablespoon cornstarch
1 teaspoon orange zest

COBBLER TOPPING
2 cups all-purpose flour
1 teaspoon salt
1 tablespoon baking powder
⅓ cup granulated sugar
½ cup (1 stick) cold unsalted butter, cubed
¾ cup heavy cream, plus more for brushing
Turbinado sugar

Preheat the oven to 350°F and place a 10-inch cast iron skillet over medium heat.

Combine the plums, brown sugar, red wine, cornstarch and orange zest in the skillet. Bring to a simmer and cook for 6 to 8 minutes, or until the plums are tender and the sauce thickens. Remove from heat and set aside.

In a bowl, whisk together the flour, salt, baking powder and sugar. Use a fork or pastry blender to incorporate the butter into the flour mixture, until it resembles a coarse crumble.

Slowly pour in the heavy cream, reserving about a tablespoon for brushing. Mix until the dough begins to clump together.

Evenly place large lumps of dough on top of the filling in the skillet. Brush the dough with heavy cream and sprinkle with turbinado sugar.

Bake the cobbler for 35 minutes, or until the topping is golden brown. Cool slightly, then serve with a scoop of vanilla ice cream or fresh whipped cream.

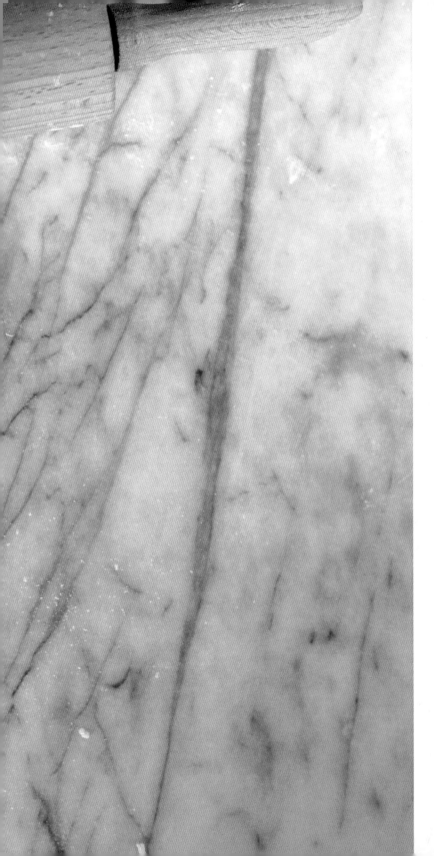

So easy, my kid could do it!

n May of 2013, I had my son, Nolan. Saying that he changed my priorities is an understatement. Before having him, I could spend hours on end in the kitchen without a care in the world. Just me and my first love, my glossy red stand mixer, baking to our hearts' content. But something happened once that little man arrived: I stopped having time. My days quickly shifted into fulfilling a much more important role: that of being a mom. I would eventually get back to spending hours in the kitchen, but certainly fewer than I did pre-baby.

This chapter highlights a few of my favorite recipes that are not just easy, they won't consume your entire day. These recipes are fun to eat, fun to make and the perfect excuse to get your kids involved in the kitchen. I'm a big fan of family participation, but make sure you keep an eye on the little ones. If they're anything like my son, they'll attempt to devour a stick of butter before you can turn on the oven.

BREAKFAST KEBABS

BERRY HONEY BUTTER

SWEETHEART HAND PIES

CITRUS CONFETTI COOKIES

SUGAR & SPICE TWISTS

CHOCO-NANA TART

Keep the pancakes and French toast bites warm until assembling skewers in a 200°F oven.

BREAKFAST KEBABS

YOU'LL NEED:

Silver Dollar Banana Pancakes (see recipe)

French Toast Bites (see recipe)

Berries, such as strawberries, raspberries
and blackberries

Confectioners' sugar for dusting

Maple Syrup

Several Skewers

Makes 8-10

SILVER DOLLAR BANANA PANCAKES

1 cup all-purpose flour

2 tablespoons granulated sugar

1 teaspoon baking powder

½ teaspoon salt

1 cup milk

1 egg

1 teaspoon vanilla extract

2 tablespoons unsalted butter, melted

1 banana, peeled and thinly sliced

FRENCH TOAST BITES

4 eggs

1 cup milk

2 teaspoons vanilla extract

1 teaspoon cinnamon

Pinch of salt

1 loaf dense, rustic bread, cut into 1½-inch cubes
(I like semolina or even cinnamon-raisin)

The idea of breakfast kebabs came up over a debate with my husband. We couldn't agree on whether to serve pancakes or French toast for a brunch hosted at our apartment. I was Team Pancake, mostly because I support anything with the word "cake" in it; my husband was adamant that French toast was the way to go. Marriage is about compromise, right? So I suggested we make both in miniature form, and the Breakfast Kebab made its debut. Whether you're entertaining for brunch or just seeking a creative Sunday breakfast for your family, these kebabs will certainly satiate any sweet tooth. Silver dollar banana pancakes, fluffy French toast and fresh fruit, all topped with confectioners' sugar and syrup? *That's a well-rounded meal!*

Combine all the ingredients except the banana slices in a bowl and whisk until all the lumps are gone.

Butter a nonstick frying pan and place over medium heat.

Use a teaspoon to spoon batter onto frying pan and quickly top with a banana slice. Flip after about 30 seconds, or when several bubbles have formed in the batter.

Cook on the other side for another 30 seconds, then set pancakes aside until assembly.

In a large bowl, beat the eggs, milk, vanilla, cinnamon and salt. Add bread cubes, stir to coat and let them soak up the egg mixture.

Butter a nonstick frying pan and place over medium heat.

Remove bread cubes from egg mixture, shaking off excess liquid. Cook until all sides of the bread are golden brown, about 5 minutes.

To Assemble:
Wash berries and halve the strawberries. Thread fruit onto skewers, alternating with French toast cubes and pancakes.

Dust with confectioners' sugar and serve immediately with maple syrup.

BERRY
HONEY
BUTTER

While not a true dessert, this honey butter showcases one (if not the most) important ingredient in any baker's repertoire: butter. For this recipe, you must use high-quality butter. Unsalted is always best, allowing you to add just the right amount of salt. I use strawberries in this recipe, but feel free to swap in any berry. Raspberries or blackberries would taste divine. Keep things simple and serve with a crusty baguette, or let it melt atop warm homemade French toast. This butter plays well with pretty much everything.

Makes about 1½ cups

8 ounces unsalted butter, room temperature
  (I use Plugrá or Kerrygold)
1 tablespoon honey
¾ cup chopped strawberries
½ teaspoon sea salt (such as Maldon)
  plus more for topping

In the bowl of a stand mixer fitted with the paddle attachment, beat the butter for about a minute. Add in the honey, strawberries and salt, mixing just to combine.

Spoon the butter into small ramekins and sprinkle a pinch of additional salt on top.

Cover and refrigerate until butter hardens. Use within a week, or freeze for up to a month.